# A *Charmed* Life

First published in Great Britain in 2002 by
Orion Books Ltd
Orion House, 5 Upper St Martin's Lane, London WC2H 9EA

Fourth impression 2002

A CIP catalogue record for this book is available
from the British Library

ISBN 0 75285 1608

Printed by Butler and Tanner Ltd, Frome and London

This book is dedicated to Dad, Mum, my family, Derek,
Madge and Mel, with thanks and love

# Contents

# 1

# The Beginning

I was born just before dawn on 23 July 1947 in a maternity hospital in West Ham, East London, a six-pound four-ounce baby boy, yellow with jaundice and delivered by forceps.

Maybe my reluctance to enter the world was a premonition of the incredible adventure my life would be. Certainly a moment's pause, and a few extra deep breaths at the start line, would have been welcome. David Cook, the only child of Dolly and Albert, the best mum and dad ever, was gently taken home on a trolley-bus to a flat in a house in Redriff Road, Plaistow, to be prodded, tickled, picked up and welcomed by various aunts, uncles, friends and relations.

My mother, ever since marrying my father – who on their wedding day, obtained a pass for 24-hour leave from the Army and arrived at the church on the back of his brother George's motorbike – knew then that she would have a son and she would call him David, and here I was. I'm told I was a shy baby who smiled easily and slept well but had a habit of plonking my dinner on my head whenever Mum's back was turned. Apparently I found this very amusing and would chuckle loudly as various concoctions of baby food cascaded down my face. Obviously I had an early feel for slapstick.

Like most babies, my next job was to become mobile. I must

have worked pretty hard at this as I was up and toddling well
before the usual nine or ten months. Our flat was small and
cramped and I wore a bump constantly on my forehead from
invisible air bubbles that seemed to thwart my attempts to gallop,
and my occasional dance routines to the radio.

The nose dives and general mayhem that I produced started to
sour relations with our downstairs landlord, and when he pointed
out that children were not allowed in our flat, with its one
bedroom, kitchen and sitting-room, Mum and Dad decided to
look for another place to live. Their dream was to have their own
council flat, and of course a garden would be paradise.

The Docklands of East London had been virtually flattened by
the Blitz, and the Government had embarked on a programme of
quickly building cheap housing for the displaced East Enders. So
Mum and Dad were put on a very long waiting list for rented
accommodation in one of these strange new vertical housing estates.

Homeless and waiting, we went to live in Canning Town with
my mother's sister, Aunt Ellen, Uncle Bob and their little daughter Rose. Although it was a council house it had a small garden
and we were made most welcome. Time dragged on as we waited
and waited for a place of our own. My father, after his 'demob'
from the Army, was working hard as a docker in the Royal
Docks, and Mum was working hard trying to keep me amused,
spending as much time as possible out of the house and out from
under the feet of our relations.

She would push me mile after mile in a second-hand pushchair,
visiting local parks and the hubbub of Rathbone Street Market, a
colourful and fascinating place for a teething two-year-old. The
market was spread over a large area which had been bombed in
the war. There were shops, stall-holders and traders who would
simply spread out a blanket on the waste ground and sell stuff.
You could buy anything there from beetroot to second-hand
bikes, and everybody from miles around did.

Meanwhile, a year or so on, there was still no word from the council, and with no prospect of leaving the housing list, my parents thought we had outstayed our welcome with Ellen and Bob. So, after a brief discussion between both families, it was decided that Aunt Ellen would ask us to leave, making us in fact homeless, and Dad would speak to the council and hopefully some kind of action on the home front would be forthcoming. The council responded with an offer for my mother and me of a place in what I suppose was a modern equivalent of the workhouse.

Forest House, James Lane was an institution for the homeless and mentally ill. Mum and I were given a curtained cubicle with just a single bed and a small cabinet. Although I was only two years old, I still have some memories of the place. The curtains had pink roses on them, there were long green and cream corridors with that kind of hospital smell lingering in the air, and there was lots and lots of noise. My father paid our rent for us, it was eighteen shillings a week, while he was forced to stay with his sister Ivy in not too far away Barking. It was a depressing time for Mum and Dad. I know my father's pride was hurt.

Our new home was in a place called Whipps Cross, near Wanstead Flats, surrounded by what I thought was countryside, a rural oasis on the edge of East London, where a small herd of cows roamed between the traffic and the Flats. I don't know who they belonged to, but local folklore would have it that in the early days of rationing the Kray brothers would bump the odd cow off and flog it to local butchers to supplement their income.

At Forest House, which seemed massive to me, the floor we lived on was full of women and children crammed into these small cubicles, with one kitchen shared by all. I really don't know how they coped, but they did. Mum and I would have our breakfast at seven a.m., then leave, returning at about five p.m. and count the minutes to Dad's visit after work.

I kind of liked it there. I remember vividly a poor inmate on the floor below us being strapped down as he had an epileptic fit, and the occasional child-like mentally ill patient trudging the corridors or singing loudly. The whole place had a surreal atmosphere which fascinated my young mind. There was a kind and friendly inmate who asked if I would like some conkers. Mum said she thought I might and was amazed when he returned in the evening with a coal sack full of them. Another gentleman persuaded Dad he could fix his watch, which was losing time, and dutifully returned it in a hundred pieces.

Although I was happy enough, it was a sad and difficult time for my parents. Mum and I would spend the day wandering around Wanstead Flats, or we would catch a bus to my grandmother's in Stratford for a cup of tea and a chat.

Nan was Mum's mother and a wonderful lady, a real character. She had struggled all her life to bring up her seven children, married twice and had done a terrific job keeping together a group of children with different mothers or fathers, but she loved them all. She was the second wife of Mum's father, an Irish travelling tinker man. He had died before I was born, but the gypsy blood still ran strong and proud in Mum's family. Mum told me that when my grandfather's first wife died and Grandad married my nan, the first wife's mother came over from Ireland and stood outside my nan's house cursing her. Dressed in a black kind of flamenco/Victorian dress, she brandished the silver sovereign necklace she was wearing around her neck, saying that she had money and that my nan would always be penniless – and so she always was, spending a lot of time at the pawnbroker's and working her fingers to the bone.

Six long months had gone by and there was still no news of a place of our own. My mother was so down at this point that she even contemplated jumping from the fire escape next to our cubicle and ending the nightmare. Dad meanwhile carried this empty feeling that he had let us down. Even then I could sense the sadness in them both.

I was three years old when the news we had prayed for came at last. Our own place, a council prefab in Hooper Road, Custom House, and it even had a garden. It may well have looked like a Nissan hut from the Second World War, but to us it was Buckingham Palace. We said goodbye to our friends at Forest House and moved into Hooper Road in the spring of 1951.

What a wonderful time that was. My parents were so proud. Dad laid the small garden with turf, painted and decorated. Mum made the inside like a palace, and I got in the way. The grass grew, and everything was perfect that summer. A garden of our own, a bedroom to myself and Dad and Mum happy and in love. But then the unthinkable happened.

My father would take me for bike rides on his crossbar mile upon mile. I loved it, as we pedalled past the docked ocean liners that towered over the terraced houses, past the kids playing in the streets, past the strangely dressed sailors from distant lands, past the dockers with their waistcoats and white scarves, past house-proud ladies cleaning their steps and looking a little old for their years. I would wait till Dad came home from the dock, wait as patiently as I could while he had his dinner, or tea as we called it, and ask if we could go out on the bike.

As the winter drew in he became more and more reluctant to go, saying he was tired, or had had a hard day, so I would play in the garden. Finally, after a quiet Christmas, by way of I suppose another Christmas present, he said yes, and we set off as usual to ride around the East End streets. I always wanted to go as fast as possible and we were going slowly. 'Come on, Dad.' I said, 'Let's go faster.' So my dad, being the best dad in the world, did his best but started coughing violently and said he'd had enough and we should return home. Reluctantly I agreed and we turned back.

By the time we arrived home, Dad was coughing up blood. I

was so sad as the ambulance came and took away my father, my hero and my best friend. I can remember it like it was yesterday.

My Father had contracted tuberculosis and was taken on New Year's Eve to spend three months in Victoria Chest Hospital in Hertfordshire. Just as we were together for a perfect little Christmas, we were torn apart.

Life without Dad was pretty bleak. Of course Mum was there, she always had been, but I missed him a lot. The visits to Hertfordshire used to take us a whole day, and sadly when we got there to see Dad we weren't allowed to go near him or touch him as TB is very contagious. Dad had a big photograph of me by his bed. I remember wishing it really could be me by the bed instead of the photograph.

Back in Hooper Road, with Mum now working as a cleaner in a local pub, I was enrolled at the Dockland Settlement nursery school in Canning Town. The school was run by the Reverend David Sheppard, whom even as a small child I recognized as someone special. I was told he had been a famous cricketer, so I was impressed, not that I really understood cricket at that time. The only sport I'd played was football, either with the other kids in the street or in a kickabout with Dad in the garden.

I found the nursery a little intimidating. Having been an only child with a fair amount of time alone to daydream, now I was suddenly surrounded by thirty or more boys and girls with seemingly endless energy, all of them in a manic rush to claim and hold on to the best of the limited toys available. It made me withdrawn.

It's still a part of my character today. Although I'm a performer there's a major part of me that is an introvert. Perhaps I perform to communicate.

After a few weeks as an outsider, I started to make a few friends, one of whom, David Elliot, is still a friend today. Once I learned to battle with the rest I enjoyed my time there.

It was disappointing some afternoons, as Mum would pick me up and I would relate the adventures of the day, not to see Dad. After all there are some things you want to tell Dad about, like the Reverend David Sheppard saying you were good at football and cricket in the playground, or the way you stood up to a bully, or how Mavis Heart had tried to kiss you. You know, men's stuff. But Dad was soon coming home and we were moving up in the world, in more ways than one.

The council had given us a new flat on the third floor of Avondale Court, Canning Town, and soon after Dad came home we moved in. It was brilliant, it had two bedrooms, a lounge, a kitchen and, best of all, a balcony that overlooked a playground and some grass bits that you weren't allowed on. I liked being up in the air. Our flat was on the top floor, so you could see the cranes of the docks in the distance and two giant chimneys shaped like milk bottles that belched clouds of white smoke into the East End sky. I thought they were cloud-making machines, but Dad said they belonged to the local power station.

Dad was pleased to be home and was in good spirits, though he looked older to me and spent most of the time quietly convalescing. Still, it was good to look up from the playground below and get a reassuring wave or thumbs-up when I'd scored a goal.

Out of all the places we had lived, in what I suppose was a pretty unsettled early life, this was the one that always felt like home. I often drive past it these days on my way to watch West Ham United at Upton Park and, as the old song goes, 'I get a funny feeling inside of me.'

With the family back together and a new home in the sky, it was now time for my first school – Star Lane Primary. I remember my mother taking me on my first day and, as the other children fussed and cried, I think she was surprised by my worldliness. 'Bye, Mum. See you later,' I said and in I went.

Star Lane was a typical old Victorian school. Built on three floors, it looked massive. There were two playgrounds and a large playing field at the back. I loved it there from the very start.

Days in the infant school were spent playing, punctuated with gentle lessons for reading, writing and sums. I remember sunny afternoons when temporary beds were lined up under the trees in the playground for us little ones to have an afternoon nap. I don't think I ever really slept, but I remember the trees moving in the summer breeze, the blue skies and the sound of passing cars, horsedrawn carts and rumbling lorries.

Talking of horses and carts, milk men used them to deliver the milk at that time. One morning on my way to school I remember one horse taking a liking for another which culminated in a cart being turned on its side, broken bottles and puddles of milk everywhere. The local cats thought it was Christmas.

I suppose during our lives we all come across people who have a strong influence on us. At Star Lane there were two or three teachers who influenced me. Firstly the head teacher, Miss Hood. She was a wonderful lady who had the respect and love of so many of her pupils in the many years she spent at the school. You somehow wanted to do well for her and you were proud of the school, which meant of course that when you played for or represented the school you did your best.

There was an English teacher who in fact was Welsh. Mr Lloyd instilled in me a real interest in the subject. He had big, bushy, grey eyebrows, and while other lesser teachers would rant and rave to discipline us wayward lot, with him just a lift of an eyebrow in your direction was more than enough to restore order. He would weave spells with his magical Welsh voice and his twinkling blue eyes, and without doubt was the best teacher I had throughout my chequered school life.

One of the upsetting things about state schools in recent times is the lack of sport. Cricket, football and rugby to a certain extent have become a luxury, and cricket and rugby are in danger of becoming elitist sports only played by private schools. This was not so in the 1950s, and at Star Lane football and cricket were played by all the boys, while the girls played netball and rounders.

We were also lucky to have a couple of good sports masters. There was Mr Morgan, another Welshman, who was much feared – in fact regarded by us as a psychopath – and an elderly teacher, Mr Dunlop. While most of the A teams preferred Mr Dunlop's approach, I think I needed the sergeant major-type motivation of Mr Morgan to get me running endlessly round that wet and cold playing field. You worked hard, you did your best. There was really no alternative.

I have always loved sport, and although football was my passion, I've enjoyed playing nearly every sport over the years. I'm sure that in many ways being a part of a team, wanting to win, but accepting the losses in a sportsmanlike way, helped build my character and probably prepared me later on for the odd auditions I didn't get.

School days were good, and life in Avondale Court was filled with friends and happiness. Even better, my father was getting stronger and couldn't wait to return to work. Dad wanted to go back to the docks, but was not fit enough to load or unload tons of cargo as he did before, so he decided to take various exams to become a tally clerk. A tally clerk is of course less physical, logging cargo on and off ships by means of paper work instead of brute force.

Dad was the youngest of thirteen children. His father, a stern and very Victorian Scotsman from Greenock, near Glasgow, never called my dad by his name, which was Albert, but referred to him as 'One Too Many'. It was only poverty that had prevented my father from taking up an offer of a place at university, so he passed the exams with flying colours and proudly re-entered the docks as a tally clerk.

It was very important for my father. He hated being an invalid, despised having to take sickness benefit. Now you could see his dignity and self-esteem begin to return.

After a few shaky years there was some order returning to our family. Dad was back at work, Mum was cleaning the pub and sometimes, in the evening, playing the piano there. Although self-taught, Mum played the piano quite well in a sort of Winifred Attwell style. These were the days when men still whistled and people would have singsongs around the piano. Many times a couple of friends and I would sit outside the pub with our lemon-ade and crisps serenaded by the locals' renditions of Al Jolson or more current popular songs. Music was live and very social. Our flat was always full of music, as the radio, or wireless as it was called, was constantly on. We didn't have a television at that time, and the current favourites would drift around the kitchen courtesy of the BBC Light Programme.

I was now seven or eight, and Mum had taken a full-time job in an electrical shop, so I had become a 'latchkey kid'. I would come home from school about four o'clock, stick my hand through the letterbox where the door key hung on a piece of string, and let myself in. Mum would leave me some bread and jam and orange juice. I'd grab it and dart downstairs to the play-ground to play football, or whatever was going, and come in reluctantly when called for tea around seven when my parents got home. I was becoming quite an independent chap – perhaps a bit too much so.

I remember one night in October, when the neighbourhood was preparing for what I thought was the best night of the year – Fireworks Night. All around, on patches of wasteland flattened by the Blitz, big bonfires were being built. Some of them looked like mountains. There was a kind of anarchic carnival atmosphere in the air. In fact it was quite dangerous, as there was none of the respect for fireworks that people have now, and no organized displays. The firework code back then was light a banger and throw it.

Boys would fire rockets along the street. It seemed much more fun than shooting them into an empty sky. We would have firework fights. One particularly sinister piece of kit was made from a small pipe nailed on to a block of wood. The pipe would be filled with gunpowder from emptied bangers then loaded with a ball bearing, ready for lighting and firing. I've seen one of these blow apart the bottom half of someone's front door.

We thought sparklers were fun to throw at each other. I got into terrible trouble for setting fire to a girl's hair, even though it was a wonderful throw from the third floor, scoring a direct hit on her bonce.

That was nothing, however, compared with a moment of madness that would shock and almost blow up half of Canning Town. I had gotten hold of a box of coloured matches, nice things but a little boring – you light them and they just burn different colours. I was wandering the streets with the matches burning a hole in the pocket of my short trousers, and I walked past a piece of wasteland where lorries used to be parked overnight before unloading in the docks nearby. There were about eight of them parked up, mostly covered in canvas, and full of stuff for abroad.

The drivers would stay in local hostels or bed and breakfast places and join the queue early the following morning to unload at the docks. So here they were, these giants of the road, still and silent, smelling of petrol, oil and canvas. I walked around them, climbed over them and then remembered the matches.

In a moment of madness, I undid one lorry's petrol cap, lit a match and threw it in. Nothing happened. I tried again. Why I was so intent on this crazy experiment I'll never know. Another match – again nothing. 'I know,' I thought, 'I'll light a match, put it back into the box, which will light all the matches, and drop the lot down the petrol pipe.'

Mission accomplished. A twenty-foot flame shot out from the petrol tank. Shocked at its power and scared of the consequences,

I ran as I'd never run before. Bang! The first lorry exploded. Looking behind, I saw the next lorry catch fire, and by the time I had run the quarter mile or so back home the night sky was filled with smoke and lit up by my reckless deed.

'Are you all right?' asked Mum, as I made it to our door.

'Yeah,' I said. 'We were having a race.' In fact I only told Mum the truth about ten years ago. She was horrified to think that her little boy was the mystery arsonist in what the *Stratford Express* called at the time 'The Canning Town Arson Attack'.

Although in retrospect what I did was nuts, I'd like to put it down to an enquiring mind. Yes, I suppose mischief could have replaced my middle name – Albert – but I couldn't have been that bad. After all, I was a sixer in the Cubs.

I enjoyed my time in the Cubs and dibbed and dobbed with the best of them. I remember going on a two-week camping trip to Herne Bay in Kent, sleeping under bell tents and searching for a ghost in nearby Reculver. The group was run by 'Baloo', a rotund and genial man called Mr Minter, who did his best to keep us entertained and under control. I suppose my first brush with showbiz happened at a talent contest that was organized at the camp. Although it was completely out of character, I entered it. I mimed to Elvis's 'All Shook Up' and came second to a kid who sang 'She'll Be Coming Round the Mountain' out of tune.

# 2

# Memories of Hopping and Football

When I say hopping I don't mean jumping up and down. In the mid Fifties, many of the women and children of East London still carried on the tradition of hop picking in Kent. Offering a few weeks in the real countryside, hop picking was looked upon as both the only holiday available and a way of making a small amount of money, and was something my mother and nan loved.

We would go with a few belongings on the back of a lorry, and drive through the Blackwall Tunnel and into darkest Kent – it was brilliant. I especially liked the lorry ride. Mostly women and children would pack the back of the lorry, surrounded by pots and pans, bags and suitcases as we headed through south-east London and into the Garden of England. It was great fun, rumbling through the villages and countryside, the wind in our faces, like a small army occupying a foreign land, singing songs and waving to the locals, secure in the promise of a new adventure.

After a two or three hour drive we arrived at our destination in Rolvenden, Kent. It was very exciting to pull up at the farm, with its outbuildings, huts and cow sheds that would be home for the following weeks. We were allocated our hut and given mattresses that we would fill with hay. Then we'd set about making our small shed as comfortable as possible. There was a communal wash-house, not unlike the one in Forest House, and the true togetherness of families – everyone watching out for everyone else.

For us kids, this was a different world. The stars which shone so much brighter than in London, the sights and smells of the countryside, all so different, walking over fields in the evening to the village pub for crisps and lemonade. The kids would play outside, then walk back through the starlit fields. Later we'd listen to the grown-ups singing around an open fire as we lay on our hay-smelling mattresses with an oil lamp flickering above, as we gently fell asleep.

I must admit, I didn't do much hop picking. Occasionally I would help Nan or Mum fill up a bushel, but most of my time was spent having fun, climbing trees and running wild. One afternoon I actually got chased by a bull. I ran so fast I lost my prized beret off my head, jumped clean over a five-foot fence and never went back to claim the beret. That bull was mean.

My favourite time was when Dad and most of the other menfolk would come and visit at the weekends. It was brilliant – football matches, fishing and late nights outside the pub. Now and then we met up with a few of our gypsy relatives who would work in the fields with us. There was an Uncle Levi, who told wonderful stories. He was a tall and handsome man with jet black hair slicked back with liquid paraffin, thankfully a non-smoker, he had a dark complexion and twinkling eyes. I remember him telling me that the natural things in life were the important things: not material things, but sunsets, the countryside, nature and good health. I was more interested in red sports cars at the time – but how right he was.

To a scruffy little Londoner, the hop picking trips seemed to last for ever. As much as I enjoyed them, it was exciting at the end of the season to load on to the lorry again and head home for the Smoke, remembering new friends, but looking forward to seeing old friends and familiar places.

The East End was slowly changing. Much of the wasteland, or debris as we called it, was being built on. High-rise blocks of flats were appearing and a steady flow of immigrants was moving in. We were used to sailors from distant lands with their different clothes and different faces, but now Pakistanis and West Indians were moving in as our neighbours.

This didn't worry me, they were welcome. But to the older East Enders the influx represented a threat; they were suspicious and fearful and the changes worried them. This undercurrent of resentment would now and then erupt into violence. I remember a running battle between some Teddy Boys and some West Indian boys armed with knives, chains, sticks and bottles. It was a sickening sight.

I was now ten years old and approaching the dreaded Eleven Plus which, as you may know, was an exam we all took which determined our future. If you passed you went to a grammar school, but if you failed you were condemned to a state secondary school and a life as factory fodder. Throughout all my time at Star Lane I had been in the A class, and looked a sure bet to pass. The only problem I had was that the grammar school played rugby for half the winter term, whereas the state secondary school played football for the whole winter term and therefore had a much better football team. As football was my life at that time, I had to avoid the risk of passing the exam.

The Eleven Plus was upon us, a week of serious stress. Our usually friendly and helpful teachers had turned into concerned undertakers at a scholastic funeral. Solemnly, the maths paper was passed out. Mr Milner our maths teacher had tried his best with us, but I sensed in him a serious lack of optimism as he moved from desk to desk, his shoes creaking, then broke the deathly silence of the exam room with that daunting phrase, 'You may now start.' I looked at the sky through the large Victorian window and reflected on this football versus a better education question. I scanned the exam paper for a minute or two, drew a picture of Popeye on it and dutifully failed.

Mum and Dad were a little surprised at my failure, but I was going to Shipman County Secondary School and they played good football, so for me it was a result. I left Star Lane with a tinge of sadness but looked forward to the summer holiday.

The six-week holiday was spent in the usual way, banging about the local streets and parks, sliding down the sewer bank on sheets of metal at great speed and generally finding as many adventures as possible to fill the days.

One outing I recall was a bike ride to Abbey Woods, south of the Thames. My Dad had bought me a second-hand bike from Petticoat Lane for my eleventh birthday, a Gresham Flier. With three friends, I decided to cycle to Woolwich, catch the ferry and explore South London. We finished up in Abbey Woods, having heard that the hills there were really steep and you could go down them at about a hundred miles an hour, without peddling – much too good a prospect to miss. As the famous four lined up at the top of a particularly steep hill, Roger Chapman said we should swap bikes. The plan was approved and I got one with a fixed wheel. Shirts off and ready for the big one, we took off. If I wasn't breaking the sound barrier, it certainly felt like it. I was in the lead and the bike was airborne, my legs in the air and barely in control … a bend! A ditch! … I needed to brake. With the pedals whizzing round in a blur I tried to jam my sandals down on them to slow down – a big mistake. Over the crossbar I went and into the biggest clump of stinging nettles ever. The pain was terrible. I was covered from head to toe in stings. Roger was worried about his bike as I rose out of the nettles like Frankenstein's monster.

It was now the last week of what had seemed to be an endless summer holiday and our thoughts were turning to the new school, Shipman County Secondary School. Situated in Custom House, about a mile from our flat, Shipman was a typical old Victorian school, similar to Star Lane but bigger. The switch did not involve much preparation – there were no school books or uniform to buy. In fact the school uniform for the boys consisted of jeans, leather jackets and boots with steel toe-caps, and the school books still showed India coloured pink as part of the British Empire.

With Mum and Dad at work, arrangements were made for me to walk to school with a boy called Mike Newell, who was a year or so older than me. Mike lived in a ground-floor flat in our block. I wasn't in Mr and Mrs Newell's good books of late, having hit a cricket ball through their sitting-room window, partly demolishing their radiogram. Mike was a good friend, though, and he thought my cover drive was a great shot.

We set off at about eight o'clock for the walk to school, through Rathbone Street Market, which was waking up for another busy day, through the streets to Prince Regent Lane, and into the school playground. Then Mike immediately disowned me. I suppose he had to take stock of his street cred and couldn't be seen hanging out with a tiddler like me.

The first thing that struck me was the size of the boys there. Of course I was in the youngest year, but some of the fourth years looked like men. Not to mention the girls. They had all the right things in the right places.

I was nervous and edgy. This was a rough school with a reputation for violence, academically weak but with strong football sides and the best boxing team in London. Talking of boxing, the famous boxing manager Terry Lawless was an old friend of my father's from the docks, and the Royal Oak pub, so famous in boxing circles, was at the end of our street. West Ham has produced many legendary fighters, from Terry Spinks to Nigel Benn. Jimmy Tibbs used to go to Star Lane with me and went on to become one of our finest trainers. I suppose boxing offered a route out of poverty to better things.

My first week at my new school was spent getting to know my new surroundings, making new friends and circumnavigating the many school bullies and prospective world boxing champions. Unfortunately, I was sat next to a boy called Trevor who smelt of stale biscuits and seemed to have an endless stream of green stuff coming from his nose which, when Trev got excited, would bubble up in mid conversation. I hoped for better things.

They soon came in the shape of Friday afternoon games. With the school's football season about to begin, the sports teacher was looking to pick the squad to represent the school. After some ball work and a kickabout he called us in and named the team. Dave Cook was to play left half. In these days of wing backs, sweepers and diamond shapes, that position would be called a left-sided midfield player, but then it was left half. With the number six shirt proudly under my arm, I left school looking forward to our first match the next morning.

Our home ground was at Beckton Dump. All right, it doesn't have the same ring about it as Upton Park or Highbury, but it wasn't as bad as it sounds. It was a fairly desolate area, and I suppose at one time stuff was dumped there, but now it was just over-active strikers that were dumped. We kicked off at ten o'clock in our red-and-white squares shirts and black shorts. Our opponents that morning were Pretoria, which was the local school for Star Lane, so I knew most of the boys, having played along-side them in primary school. They had the brilliant Frank Lampard, who lived opposite me and went on to become an important West Ham player, as did his talented son Frank junior. Frank senior was the assistant manager under the terrific Harry Redknapp. Even so, we had a good little team and managed to edge it, 4–3.

I used to love Saturdays. Dad would finish work around lunchtime and cook sausage and mash for me when I got home. He used to buy these brilliant bangers from a butcher's called

Taylors. It was my favourite meal of the week. The two of us would sit down to eat while I gave him a match report. Dad was always very supportive even though he was never able to see any of the games.

It was about this time that I started to go to Upton Park to see West Ham. I would either travel there with a friend or go alone, catching the bus and lining up at 1.30 for the three o'clock kick-off. Upton Park in those days was all standing, and packed with dockers who would take great care of the little ones, passing us over their heads down to the front so we could see the game. It was a wonderful place, full of atmosphere and good humour, and still is.

Life at school was pretty pointless. Shipman, with its bad repu-tation, seemed to make do with a succession of second-rate teach-ers when what it really needed to turn things around were the best teachers. New faces would come and go, reeling from the lack of discipline that prevailed in the school. It can't have been easy for them. In the classroom, the done thing if you wanted to be cool and escape having your lights punched out by one of your peers, was to pay little or no attention to any well-meaning educator.

Homework was non-existent, and there was an undercurrent of anarchy in the air. The playground was an important place for the wellbeing of any pupil. Status and popularity were closely monitored and extremely fragile. The hard-nuts of the school could turn on an unsuspecting victim and make his life a torment.

I remember one boy being clumped just for wearing brown winkle pickers – a good enough reason, you may say. I disliked this aspect of school life a lot, but it was difficult to make a stand against it, as anyone who has lived through it will know. The mob can quickly turn against the do-gooder with a social conscience.

There was a crunch moment for me in the first year when I was being picked on by some second-year gang leaders. I was scared stiff, but I stood my ground and was informed, 'We're gonna have you after school.' Fights after school were nothing unusual. Participants and spectators would meet on a piece of wasteland and off it would go. As the school bell sounded for school out I was terrified, but I knew I had to go through with it or the bullying would go on and become worse. I made my way to the edge of Boot Hill, a very reluctant gladiator surrounded by a few well-wishers.

When we got there a sizeable crowd was waiting, baying for blood with shouts of 'Fight, fight.' With the moronic chants ringing in my ears, I saw my opponent, their main man, Lenny. Len and I squared up to each other, Len had a big reputation, he could swear with great venom and was also able to spit through his front teeth a great distance. 'Fight, fight,' went the crowd.

Len went for his best shot, which whistled past my nose, followed by a steel toe-capped boot to my right thigh. I gathered we were not fighting under Queensbury Rules and nailed Len with my trusty left foot right in the plums – a strike worthy of Geoff Hurst in his prime. Len crumpled and I whacked him with a lucky punch which really hurt my hand. Len was stunned, the crowd went silent and I seemed to have won. Len's reputation was in tatters and mine was built. Even Hazel, the captain of the netball team, seemed impressed.

In truth I hated the whole thing, but from that day on I was accepted and I think generally liked. I had become physically a part of the 'in' crowd, but mentally I was full of misgivings about the negative behaviour and attitude of many of my peers.

I remember one awful case of persecution. A boy called Peter was constantly bullied, so much so that his father, a postman, came into the playground after school to sort out the bullies. When he confronted the gang they set upon him, beating him to the ground as his son looked on in tears. It was a sickening moment, and poor Peter's schooldays remained a nightmare till the end.

School disorder sometimes had a lighter side. You know the sort of thing – condoms filled with water cascading down from the top floor to the girls' playground below, or Kenny Palmer's football boots nailed to the changing-room floor.

An incident I'll never forget took place one afternoon in the science room under the unfortunate jurisdiction of Mr Dines, or 'Daddy Dines' as he was called. 'Daddy' had brought in some of his bees for us to see and had set them up nicely in a glass case by the window. The bees would fly off out of a small hole, collect pollen from the backyards of Custom House and return to the temporary glass hive.

Mr Dines proudly pointed out the workers and the larger queen bee in the middle. He then made his way to the blackboard to illustrate some information on bee stuff, leaving us all gathered around the buzzing glass case. As Mr Dines went on about workers and queens, a couple of the chaps decided to conduct their own experiment, pushing the rubber tube from a nearby Bunsen burner into the case. They blocked the hole with some chewing gum and turned on the gas. When Mr Dines came back to the bees to point out another pearl of wisdom, the bees were in a motionless clump at the bottom of the case – gassed.

'Daddy Dines' went nuts. He leapt for his cane. Then this tall, gangling man – not unlike Basil Fawlty – jumped on a chair and screamed, 'Who gassed my bees?' Now completely out of control, he went to war, smashing desks, pupils, test tubes … anything in his path. Kids were under tables, running wild, cowering in corners. Some were laughing; some more sensitive souls were crying.

It was then that I noticed one of the quieter members of the class setting fire to a broken chair. I've no idea why. Perhaps the mayhem made him snap, or he was trying to emulate the

Canning Town Arsonist. With alarm bells ringing, we joined the stampede to vacate the building and reached the relative safety of the playground, closely followed by the unfortunate Mr Dines, who by now was talking gibberish and foaming at the mouth. Suffice to say we never had science again.

We never had music or art either, and pottery wasn't even an option. Maybe not having music created an unsatisfied hunger for it later. I can't say the same for pottery.

At that time music seemed to be all around. I was now twelve, and there were skiffle groups on street corners and a bit of rock-'n'roll on the radio. I was becoming more and more interested in it, but football was still my main interest.

A big moment for me came after an away match with the school. I was approached by a scout for West Ham and asked if I would like to go for a trial at a place called Cumberland Road the following Tuesday after school. 'Yes,' I replied. It was probably the most exciting moment of my life to date.

Tuesday finally came. Nervous and excited, I caught the bus and followed the directions that Dad had given me. When I got there, there were about thirty or so boys kitted up and ready to go, and three or four coaches. Our names were ticked off and we were put into groups. After some ball work, we played a short match, after which we were summoned in by the coaches. The head coach, a kindly man called Terry, then read out a dozen or so names and called their owners to him. He spoke softly to the named ones so we could not hear. The rest of us sat on the grass, muddy and deflated. Then, to my surprise, the named group trudged off into the sunset and Terry came back to our group saying, 'Well done, boys. We would like you all to attend training same time, same place, next week.' That's how my West Ham schoolboy career started.

Occasionally first-team players would come and coach us, wonderful players like the legends Noel Cantwell, John Bond and Phil

Woosnam. Mr Bond's nickname was Muffin, which I suppose was because he had a kick like a mule and was a very stubborn defender. Anyway John worked with me a little, and one of the things he taught me was how to up-end an attacker, and then look totally innocent – my first acting lesson.

These were exciting times. We were given free passes to the home games and a feeling of belonging to the great club. Our home ground was Clapton's football ground behind the Spotted Dog pub, and this was where I scored my one and only goal for the Hammers. It was against Thurrock, and in truth it was really a clearance from just over the halfway line which bounced over the goalkeeper's head and into the goal, but of course I made out it was exactly what I meant to do as I went about my slightly muted celebration.

Life at this time was pretty busy for me, as I also had a couple of part-time jobs. I was working for a man who doubled as Fagin in Rathbone Street Market selling ex-Army clothes. And on Monday, Wednesday and Friday nights I'd stand on the corner selling newspapers – *Star*, *News* and *Standard*. The man that ran the Newspaper Mafia, Harry I think his name was, had an amazing sales cry. I've no idea what he actually shouted, but it started sort of like Louis Armstrong and finished more like Miss Piggy. As it boomed around the foggy streets of Canning Town, it seemed to be as much a part of life there as the ships' foghorns and the buzz and clatter of the trolley bus wires.

# 3

# Red Lights and Rum and Blacks

In my thirteenth summer some fundamental changes began to happen, changes that would shape my life. Puberty and Girls. Although I was very shy of them, girls were starting to become interesting. Meanwhile the gang I used to run with was starting to look for fresh pastures. Regular gang fights were still an unfortunate part of my life. Waging war on other youth clubs, sorties into other local districts, making our presence felt to enhance the reputation of the Canning Town Boys – it was something I was sadly swept along by. Although most of my logic told me this was senseless, I suppose the need in boys for some kind of tribalism is normal, and being part of the gang seemed a safer option than being outside it and becoming a possible victim.

It was the collective restlessness of us rebels without too many causes that led the boys and me to plan a trip to London's West End, a trip that would have a pivotal effect on my future. We decided to catch the bus and experience the joys of Soho. There were about nine or ten of us looking cool in our Italian suits and button-down shirts, not to mention those chisel-toe shoes – I said don't mention them!

We boarded the bus and hit London's red-light district at around eight p.m. Tommy and Freddie, two of the older boys

24

who were about fifteen, led the posse. We walked through the narrow atmospheric streets, past the strip joints, dirty book shops and everything else that a cosmopolitan sleaze centre has to offer. It was pretty exciting and a little scary.

After an hour or so and a trip to a coffee bar where you sat on coffins, a plan was hatched actually to go into a strip joint. So, looking pretty dapper and probably older than our years, with trepidation we found one we fancied. The Greek Cypriot on the door seductively beckoned to us and in we went. Tommy couldn't wait. He always seemed a little over-sexed to me, but perhaps I was envious of his confidence with the opposite sex. Mind you, if all his supposed conquests were genuine Tommy would have had trouble walking.

We paid at the door and went up some stairs. At the top of the stairs we entered a smoky room with red lights. There was a bar in the corner and a small stage with a few rows of old cinema seats facing it. These were populated by three or four shadowy and seedy-looking men. One looked a lot like our headmaster, Mr Bell, but I don't think it was. Music was playing but nobody was on stage. There was a lady in hot pants and make-up behind the bar and a waitress in the corner having a fag.

We were not really sure of the code of conduct, never having been to a place like this before, but when the hot-panted waitress finished her fag we ordered some drinks. It seemed to be compulsory. 'A rum and black,' I said in my most grown-up voice and, just as I took my first sip, a ripple of slightly embarrassed applause sounded and Lulu hit the stage. I didn't want to say anything, but Lulu bore a striking resemblance to Roger Foster's mum.

Bumping and grinding to Guy Mitchell's 'She Wears Red Ribbons and a Hula Hula Skirt', Lulu progressed through her routine with a blank look on her face, very few clothes on, and not a red ribbon in sight. 'This is great,' said Kenny Palmer. I wasn't so sure. I kept thinking: 'I wonder if she likes doing this?'

Lulu then picked up the clothes she had taken off and shuffled off in her G-string.

Then there was another gap in the proceedings. It seemed the girls went round working in one club after another, which made stage management a little haphazard as it left twenty or thirty minutes between performances. We had another drink while eagerly awaiting the next artiste. Finally she came through the shiny backdrop and off we went again. I can't remember who she was introduced as, but she looked a bit like Doris Day, just not as good-looking. Tom was in love, and I was certainly interested.

After Doris we waited and waited, and then, with a group feeling that we had been had, we decided to make a run for it without paying for the drinks. We flew down the stairs *en masse*. The bloke on the door tried to rugby tackle me, but thankfully I managed to side-step him and we were free.

Now men of the world, we walked knowingly through the bustling streets laughing and satisfied that they hadn't 'taken us for a ride' when, as we turned a corner, a big grey Jaguar pulled alongside with windows wound down and three men inside. The man in the front passenger seat looked at me, smiled, and then growled and produced a shiny butcher's hook.

'Run!' I shouted. Just then the man in the back seat unveiled a shotgun from under a cloth. We made off in all directions.

Jimmy Anderson and I ran down a back alley, climbed over a ten-foot wall at record speed and ran through some market stalls to apparent safety.

We didn't see the rest of the boys again that night, but as the gentlemen in the Jag seemed to have taken a shine to me and Jim, we presumed they had got away unscathed.

As the dust settled, Jimmy and I nervously made our way back to the bright lights. We walked down Wardour Street, checking every car that went by and keeping an eye open for the rest of the chaps. Then we saw a queue of people waiting outside a club called The Flamingo. The music coming out of the place was terrific, so we decided to go in.

The Flamingo was an all-night rhythm and blues club full of black American soldiers on leave and the best music I had ever heard. It made Guy Mitchell's 'Hula Hula Skirt' song sound like a bunch of coconuts. Like the star over Bethlehem it was showing me where my path lay. I decided there and then that I had to be a musician.

I was really struck with the power of 'the blues' and 'rhythm and blues'. The atmosphere. The musicianship of Georgie Fame and the Blue Flames. Everything was special. The records the club played. The energy of the place. I felt like I had discovered the meaning of life – something that Lulu had failed to do for me. These were not minor stirrings; this was the answer. Wide-eyed I surveyed the instruments and musicians that made this wonderful sound. The drums immediately captured my imagination – you hit them, they answered back, they were the rock the rest was built upon. I wanted to be a drummer.

We stayed till they closed at around 4.30 in the morning. Having spent all our money we started the long walk home, tired but excited. We talked about becoming musicians, starting a band and playing at The Flamingo. Jimmy was going to play the trumpet and I was going to be a drummer, and as the sun rose over the East End I found a new direction and a new beginning.

When I finally arrived home it was about seven-thirty and Dad was in the kitchen making a morning cup of tea. 'Hello, mate,' he said. 'Enjoy yourself last night?'

'Yeah, it was neat,' I replied.

I couldn't tell him about the strip joint skirmish or the wonderful Flamingo all-nighter. After all, I'd told my parents I was staying at a friend's house in Custom House, so they wouldn't worry. But I was plucking up courage to hit him with the 'Dad, I want to be a drummer' idea.

I was aware it wasn't going to be easy to sway any decision my way. Apart from the idea coming out of the blue, the walls of the council flat were pretty thin and drums were pretty loud. We sat down in the front room.

'You look tired, son.'

'I am a bit,' I said. 'I didn't sleep much last night.'

I was so excited about the prospect of being a musician that I couldn't hold back. I felt I had to bite the bullet. 'Dad,' I said. 'You know I wanted to be a footballer?'

'Yes,' he said.

'Well what I'd really like to be is a drummer.'

To my surprise the bombshell I thought I was dropping didn't explode. Dad responded in his usual positive way. 'Sounds like a good idea,' he said. 'But you would have to keep the noise down. I'll speak to Mum.' I really wanted to go on about the music, the all-nighter, everything, but I knew I was supposed to have been staying at a friend's. I hated hiding the truth, but this time I thought honesty was not the best policy.

Over the next week or so I kept up the drum pressure. I had some money saved from the newspaper and market jobs I'd been doing, and every night I went to gaze at the window of a second-hand music shop in Barking Road, where there was a snare drum which I could just afford. All I needed was the nod.

Dad was traditionally an easier target than Mum. Mum tended to think things through a bit more. 'We'll see' became her stock reply. I suppose she wanted to make sure this drummer idea was not just a passing fad. In the meantime, I'd set up various biscuit tins, cushions and ash trays to resemble a drum kit and bashed away at them with a pair of knitting needles, as the football sat in the hall, unkicked.

One evening, as I played along to the radio, Dad said, 'How much is this drum you want?'

'It looks really good,' I said. 'And it's only a fiver.'

'Come on then, let's go and look at it.'

'Thanks, Dad,' I said, and off we went. I grabbed the seven pounds and some change I'd saved and we made our way to the music shop window just before closing time. There it was, shining, white mother of pearl – waiting to be played – and it came with a stand. In we went.

I was mesmerized; this was Aladdin's cave. Drum sets, saxophones and guitars glittered all around us. I pointed to the snare drum in the window and the assistant, who looked a bit like Johnny Cash, went to get it.

'Thanks, Dad,' I said again.

'You're paying for it,' he reminded me.

Johnny Cash returned and put the drum and stand on the counter. 'Do you want to try it?' he said, and handed me a pair of sticks. I gave the drum a whack – it sounded worse than my biscuit tin at home.

'Is it supposed to sound like that?' Dad sounded doubtful.

'Well, for that kind of money,' came the reply.

'What else have you got?' Dad asked.

Johnny pointed to a snare and stand for fifteen pounds. 'Try this one,' he said. I obliged and it sounded like a real drum.

'That seems better,' said Dad. 'Do you want that instead?'

'Yes please. It's brilliant,' came my gobsmacked reply. We bought some brushes, sticks and a rubber practice pad and headed home. It was probably the best present I've ever had.

Now the fact that Mum and Dad had gone along with their little drummer boy didn't mean that they enjoyed the racket I made – any more than the neighbours did. Even though Dad was not a big fan, his respect for personal choice and freedom was illustrated by an incident involving our downstairs neighbour, Mr Johnson. Dad had stipulated that I was only allowed to practise from 4.30 till six p.m. and that I had to use the rubber practice pad as much as possible. So this is what I did. Even so, it was too much for Mr Johnson. If the drumming didn't stop, he said he would to write to the council and get us evicted. Now I think that secretly Dad disliked the racket I kicked up as much as Mr Johnson did, but felt we were being perfectly reasonable and that Mr Johnson's bangings on the ceiling from below with his broomstick was an assault on personal freedom. The situation got worse, and, after a cold stand-off, one fateful night Mr Johnson blew his top and declared war.

I was practising paradiddles (a drum rudiment) in the bedroom when I heard shouting at the front door. It looked like Mr Johnson had gone a bridge too far this time. Dad was angry, and Mr J. made the mistake of giving Dad a prod.

The next thing I knew the two men squared up to each other. Now my dad's generation was by and large honourable in fist fights, where the rules seemed to follow those of amateur boxing. If your opponent went down, you waited till he was back on his feet – no weapons, no kicking and none of the filth of modern-day knuckles. There was an elegance to the fray, an upright dignity.

Well, there they were, two Gentlemen Jims – one fighting for peace and quiet and bigotry to all mankind, and one fighting for a young boy's dream. It was in truth a mismatch: two left jabs and a crunching right hook meant my dream lived on.

Shortly after Mr Johnson, the broomstick banger, had been silenced, I began to make more frequent trips to the West End buying all the black and obscure music I could at a specialist record shop in Charing Cross Road called Dobells, which sadly is no longer there. I would buy blues and jazz albums and, whenever I could swing it, go to watch live music at The Flamingo, The Marquee and The 100 Club. Sometimes Jim would come (he was now blowing his own trumpet), or I would drag along another mate. I was now seeing less of the gang, and although I still played football and enjoyed it, it was not the passion it once was.

A short while ago when I was the reluctant subject of *This Is Your Life*, Frank Lampard, West Ham's Assistant Manager at the time, made the kind remark that he thought I could have made it to the top as a footballer. I'm not convinced.

Around this time, 1962, Mum and Dad began actively looking to move out of East London to the more rural setting of Essex. This was a well trodden path for many East Enders. Essex Man and Woman, as the media now tend to call them, usually have close links with East London, having moved out in a bid to make a better life for their families.

My parents would follow up council house exchanges, and now and then we would go to see flats and houses in the family's grey Ford Popular – yes Dad had bought a motor, it was a cool thing. Sometimes he would let me drive down a quiet country lane, much to Mum's horror. I used to drive Dad's motorbike too, but came seriously unstuck after going for a spin down the A13.

The A13 was famously where great British bikes and Great British rockers would go for a burn-up, their Brylcreemed hair almost flowing in the wind as they did a ton and roared by in convoy to the next transport café. I've always loved motorbikes. I remember being on the back of a BSA Gold Star doing a hundred miles an hour through the Blackwall Tunnel – and that's when it was two way. The driver was a daredevil rocker called Rick, who rolled his own, never smiled, and to me at the age of eleven was everything I would like to have been.

Anyway one afternoon I borrowed, well sort of borrowed, my Dad's James Captain motorbike. The idea was to go for a spin around the block, but foolishly I kept going. I made it to the legendary A13 and opened up the throttle. The feeling of freedom was terrific. I must have been doing about 60mph in a 40mph zone when to my horror a police car pulled me over. My heart was in my mouth, a white scarf was round my face to hide the fact that I was under-age. I was well in excess of the speed limit. The friendly speed cop enquired if I knew I was speeding.

'No,' I replied in my deepest voice.

'How old are you?' he asked.

'Fourteen,' I replied with a voice that went up an octave. With a half-nelson, the officer helped me off the bike and into the police car. I received a month's ban from when I was legally able to hold a licence, that is sixteen, a twenty-pound fine and a serious telling-off from Dad. I never ventured forth again.

Over the years I've been pretty lucky and generally law-abiding with the driving. A few years later I had a Porsche 911 Turbo, black and mean and totally the wrong car for me – too fast, too soon. Anyway, I was on my way to the christening of one of my godchildren, the wonderful Claudine. I was delayed in London and hit the M3 with a vengeance and was finally stopped in Dorset for doing 160mph.

In retrospect the court hearing was quite comical, with all the newspapers in attendance. A policeman from Wiltshire took the stand and with a broad accent gave evidence in classic police-speak – 'My colleague and I were parked at a service station whereupon we heard a thunderous roar. I said, "That sounds like an unidentified object from outer space," whereupon we saw a grey blur disappear over the horizon heading south-west. We quickly gave chase but, not being able to catch up, we radioed ahead for assistance to stop the accused. When finally stopped by a road block and asked why the accused was doing speeds in excess of 160mph, he replied, "I'm late."' The courtroom collapsed in laughter. I got banned for three months and fined two thousand pounds. Definitely the wrong car for me. I sold it shortly after, but I did get to the christening on time.

After the unfortunate episode with Dad's bike had died down, my parents could see that music was a serious thing for me. I'd added more drums and cymbals and I would practise every night after school on my makeshift drum kit. Dad must have noted my commitment and asked me if I would like drum lessons, and so it began.

We had now moved from Canning Town to a ground floor flat in more countrified Chadwell Heath, a nice area next to the A12. So now the noise aspect was not such an issue. Arrangements were made for me to take some lessons at home with a really fine teacher called Eddie Freeborn. Eddie was a clean-cut gentleman who played at night in a big band and was a very good teacher.

Eddie introduced me to big band jazz and we worked through a drum tutor book full of exercises by the late and terrific Buddy Rich. Ed would sit patiently as I bossa nova'd and paradiddled away in my bedroom. I have much to thank him for.

The new flat was about five miles from school, which meant a couple of different buses. It also meant early starts and late homecomings, but as I was soon to leave school at the ripe old age of fifteen, I decided to stay at Shipman and finish my lack of education where it had begun.

Life in the fourth form at Shipman brought the odd token of responsibility. I was made a Prefect, but soon had my badge taken away for clumping someone on the stairs in a vain attempt to maintain order. The fact that he whacked me first seemed irrelevant.

With the thoughts of the flotsam and jetsam of the education system now turning to a job, the Careers Officer, or whatever he was called, came to call, interviewing us and suggesting ways to earn a crust. When my turn came and he asked what kind of career I was thinking of I didn't like to say I wanted to be a musician as I was sure he would laugh. I remembered my cousin Alfie had an impressive sounding job, so I replied 'an electrical engineer' – without having the faintest idea of what it was. In fact I still don't, but the careers bloke seemed impressed. I suppose it made a change from shop assistant or bank robber. He said he would arrange for me to take an entry exam for an apprenticeship in the summer holidays. Slightly confused I said 'Thanks.'

Dad seemed pleased with my career selection, but I was looking to play music. With the help of Eddie, I had now reached a reasonable standard as a drummer and had started to look for a semi-pro band to join. When I saw an advert in the local paper, *The Ilford Recorder*, which read 'Drummer Wanted for Trio', I showed Dad and he said, 'Give it a go.' So I rang the number and asked for Reg. Now I must say I did have suspicions that Reg and his trio would not be totally in sync with my musical ambitions – you know, The Flamingo, urban blues, the music I wanted to play. But Reg was up to a face to face so off we went to Romford for an audition, me, Dad and the drums in the car.

We found the house and rang the bell. I was right, Reg didn't look a bit like Muddy Waters, more like a spiv driving instructor with a nice line in cardigans and a pocket full of boiled sweets. 'Come in and set up,' Reg said – so I did. Dad, sensing that this was a grown-up thing for me, left me to it.

As I was putting the drums together Reg gently quizzed me about my experience, what music I liked, if I knew anything about ballroom dance music – waltzes, fox-trots and all that. Luckily, because of Eddie and his background, I could play it – but who would want to? As I finally put up my cymbals the doorbell rang and in walked the other member of the trio, Eric, who played clarinet and saxophone.

Eric was smooth and seemed to have more rings on his hand than fingers. He smelt a lot of Old Spice. Eric said 'Hi.' I'd never heard anybody say that in real life, only in American films, so thinking on my feet that this was probably a musician thing, I said 'Hi' back, whereupon Eric took out his 'liquorice stick', as he called his clarinet, and away we went, Reg on the ivories, Eric on his liquorice stick and me swishing about with my brushes, I suppose beating the skins or something, it all seemed pretty steady. They even liked my bossa nova and offered me the 'gig'. No, they didn't catch me on that one – I'd heard it before. 'Gig', which I believe is short for giggle, is musician speak for engagement.

'Great,' I said, and we sat down to peruse the forthcoming bookings. It was basically Thursday nights in a Conservative Club in Hackney and Saturday nights in a Working Man's club in Dagenham. But it was a start and I enjoyed it. Reg and Eric were good men and only got a little rattled when I started to play a cha-cha with sticks, which was my favourite part of the evening. You can get a bit frustrated swishing those brushes quietly, number after number.

It was a good feeling to be actually playing music, but it wasn't the musical direction I wanted to take, so I continued to keep an eye open for something more contemporary where I could use my sticks all night long.

The final week had arrived at school, usually a time of fond farewells between the leavers and the teachers. Not at Shipman. On the last day in recent years the police had come and searched the leavers for weapons, so that any vendettas built up over the years could be contained. I thought this was a bit over the top, but it seemed to have become an annual thing since some girls had pelted the domestic science teacher with rotten eggs a few years back.

I left Shipman School in 1962 without a twinge of sentiment, in fact I walked out the gate and never looked back.

My base now began to switch more to the area where we were living. As I was no longer travelling in to school, I began to spend less time in the East End and had started to make a few friends locally in Chadwell Heath. It was quite a different world, without the character of the area where I was born, which will always be home to me, but the air was cleaner, there were fields, and the kids from Essex were pretty cool.

A new friend called Ronnie had taken me to a local youth club, where the new boy in town was eyed with both suspicion and interest. We are not talking village hall and dances round the maypole here. I remember a massive fight at the club worthy of any western, underscored by the Crystals record 'Then He Kissed Me'. Chairs rained down and people rolled in the dust – it was just like Saturday night in the Mile End Road. I almost felt at home.

In the first week of leaving school a letter arrived from a company called Plessey's, requesting my presence at an exam for would-be apprentices. With mixed feelings I noted the time and place. My parents pointed out that this was a good opportunity. I sort of thought it was, and as Dave Brubeck or Muddy Waters had yet to knock on our door and plead with me to join their bands, there were few alternatives.

Today was the big day, I had to be at a factory in Romford, ten o'clock sharp to take the exam. I was taken to a large room with about thirty other adolescent hopefuls, seated, and we started. I can't remember too much about the content of the exam, but I do remember the bloke next to me softly mouthing the answers as he wrote them down, which, to be honest, was quite useful.

After we finished the exam we were taken on a tour of the factory, and the strangest thing happened. Lately I had been having restless dreams, not quite nightmares but fairly unpleasant, about this overpowering place, full of giant machines and noise, and when we were taken down to the machine floor there it was. I went cold. I had actually been there in my dreams. It was the strangest feeling. I didn't understand it and still don't, but it was very weird.

When the tour was over we were told we would get our results through the post in a few weeks, so I left for home with feelings of ominous destiny bouncing in my head, not sure if the dream thing meant I was supposed to do it or not supposed to do it.

Musically, I was still ticking over with Reg and Eric when I heard of an audition through my dear cousin Eileen, who over the years has been like a sister to me. She told me of a rhythm and blues band from Stratford called the Everons, meaning I suppose that they were never off! They needed a drummer. I made the call and spoke to the leader, John. He seemed interested and I was interested, so we decided to meet. John's father was a publican in Leytonstone, so we arranged to get together at the pub and have a 'jam' (luckily I knew what that meant – to play together). I got Dad to drop me and my drums off hoping for a whole session using the drum sticks.

There were three members of the Everons – John, Brian and, surprisingly, Brian's sister Sandra, who played bass guitar. John and Sandra were also a unit, so it was a pretty tight-knit group all round. I set up and we set forth. They were good, and for me it was a relief to play some blues and to hammer the drums with some volume. After an hour or so they asked me to join. I said yes and became the fourth member of the Everons.

I now felt I was on my way, playing in a contemporary group, with sticks and amplifiers – the works. I honoured my last few gigs with the trio and rehearsed two or three nights a week in a church hall in Stratford with my new band. Actually we were pretty good and soon the bookings started to come, mainly pubs, but also the odd club and wedding receptions.

The music we played was not totally what I wanted to play, there was a lack of wrist-cutting depressing blues, but then would you want that at your shindig? We also played the odd Beatles tune to keep publicans and their clientele happy, and of course a lot of Chuck Berry.

I now was enjoying playing more, I had money in my pocket and the band was starting to build a reputation. We had even secured a residency, in The Bell public house, Ilford, on Saturday and Sunday nights. I was now a semi-pro musician and it felt good.

I'm sure Mum and Dad were pleased with my progress but still harboured worries about my future and felt I should really get a proper job. These fears were eased when a letter popped through the letter box from Plessey's offering me an apprenticeship as an electrical engineer. On one hand I was pleased, but of course this reality check was not really what a fifteen-year-old would-be professional musician wanted. But hey, I passed the exam.

It was time for a family discussion. My parents understandably saw the offer of a trade and a secure future as something I should pursue. After all, if the music thing fell through I would have a trade to fall back on – whatever an electrical engineer was.

I saw their point of view and agreed to take my place in the Industrial Revolution in two weeks' time at 7.25 in the morning for the princely sum of three pounds and fifteen shillings a week. I knew the prospect of a real job would not really get in the way of the band, except of course for those early mornings after a late gig, so I prepared for my first day at the factory.

I was summoned to report to Plessey's in Ilford, a factory that made electronic stuff for the aircraft and telecommunications industries. It was a big sprawling place, but I found my way to the personnel department and was led through with two other boys to the shop floor. Here we would start to learn the ins and outs for a proposed five-year period, after which we would hopefully qualify as this mysterious electrical engineer-type person.

Working in the factory was all right. The only danger as I saw it was clocking on and clocking off. This human stampede at 7.25 a.m. and again at 5.25 p.m. was truly scary. Most of the day was spent setting up lathes for possessed piece workers who would get a bonus for a certain amount of screws made or washers pressed or other mind-numbing tasks. These people were on a mission, and anything that got in the way of them and their double time, like a sleepy apprentice, would suffer some very colourful abuse.

As well as the time at the factory, we went to college one day a week to learn our trade. I enjoyed the change, but sadly learned very little, although I'm confident I can still arc weld.

While all this went on I was still playing the drums with the band and although the shy one hid behind the cymbals had been a little slow to take much notice of girls – after all I was preoccupied with football and music – I was now becoming increasingly aware of the opposite sex. I had for a month or so noticed this ace mod girl called Carol at the local youth club and had started to make eye contact. For me, however, the leap from a glance towards each other to actually talking to her was like jumping over the moon. I envied boys who could just go over and chat girls up or even make some kind of contact – like dance. But for me it wasn't easy. Then one day Brian, our rhythm guitarist, called me to see if I wanted to go to a dance and watch another local group called The Falcons.

I said I would, and we arranged to meet outside the hall at eight. Dressed in a collarless jacket and blue jeans I waited for Brian as I watched the people go in. Suddenly I took a sharp intake of breath – she was there! Right in the middle of a group of girls going into the dance. What should I do? Hide, ignore her. Then, in a moment of courage not unlike when St George killed that Dragon, I looked Carol in the face and with knees a little weak said, 'Hello.' Her friends giggled.

'Hello, David,' she replied, looking at me, then smiled and walked on. She knew my name, I thought, she knew my name.

Brian eventually turned up wearing a rather nifty button-down shirt and mohair suit, we paid our two and sixpence and went in.

The hall was pretty full. Groups of girls were dancing to Tamla Motown records while the boys stood around trying to look cool. Brian suggested we go round and say hello to the band. Before I could answer, and to my relief, the records stopped and through a squeal of feedback The Falcons were introduced. I've never liked going backstage to see people even to this day. I always find it a little awkward and I have been reprimanded over the years for not doing so. It's not because I haven't enjoyed the performance, I suppose it's because I don't like to bother people and am sensitive to them being focused on what they are doing and what they are about to do.

The Falcons hit the stage, five of them, wearing suits and a mix of Beatle and Rolling Stone (the longer version) haircuts. They sounded pretty good and ran through band standards of the time. I was particularly impressed by their version of Screaming Lord Sutch's 'Jack the Ripper'.

Brian was going on about some kind of guitar one of them had, but my attention kept drifting back to Carol. I hadn't seen her since we went in, but then spotted her not far from the stage, dancing. Brian talked on and I was distracted, my mind spinning, knowing that if I didn't make some kind of move I might never have a better chance. After all, dances were where boys were supposed to pick up girls. Me boy – her girl, it should be easy. But it wasn't.

I spent the rest of The Falcons' set watching the band, but with half an eye on Carol who was the definite star. Two or three boys approached her to dance, but to my relief she declined. How I wished I had their courage. Half-way through 'Memphis Tennessee' by Chuck Berry she turned and spotted me – and smiled! How much more encouragement did I need?

The Falcons had finished their set, the records started, and soon the dance would finish. Brian had gone round to see the band – it was now or never. As the wind-down began, the slow records started. I took a deep breath, and with a self-conscious walk and with a mouth that hardly worked I said those immortal words, 'Do you want to dance?'

She said 'Yes' and away we went. Like most musicians, I find dancing is a bit alien to me. I've never understood that thing where people walk seemingly in control of themselves to a designated area and then explode in manic movement – weird. Anyway, there we were, dancing. Carol was good. She was doing the Bird, I think. I'm not sure what I was doing, but after a couple of Ska records a really slow one came on. This was the moment. I took her hand and we moved together, my arm around her, her hand on my shoulder, swaying gently to and fro ... it felt good.

I was experiencing for the first time the feel of a girl close to me, the smell of her perfume, the gentle touch of her body against mine. I liked it.

'Would you like a drink?' I asked. 'Yes please,' she replied, and hand in hand we made our way to a serving hatch and I splashed out on a couple of Cokes. In a moment of fizzy-drink bravado I asked if I could walk her home. Prepared for the worst but hoping for the best, I tried to look not too concerned, but broke into a smile of relief when she answered, 'Yeah, all right.' Now I was nervous. We made our way through the dying embers of the shindig and out into the warm summer night. On the way out I saw Brian, who gave me a thumbs-up and one of those knowing winks that says 'Give her one from me', which I didn't really appreciate.

As the music from the dance faded in the distance, Carol and I attempted to make embarrassed conversation but only succeeded in mind-spinning and heart-pounding silences. We turned into an alley and turned to each other. The council estate and the world stood still as, gently, we kissed. It was wonderful, no noses in the way, no banging of teeth, no tongues, but a warm, gentle, loving kiss. Not much was said as we walked with our arms around each other, slowly, to Carol's door, but I think we both felt this was something special.

We kissed and held each other in a long version of the Goodnight Kiss. I now had a Girlfriend and Carol a Boyfriend, and in the coming months we would embark together on a wonderful journey of discovery.

As I walked home I was filled with a new happiness. I even did one of those kicks in the air where you click your heels together like Charlie Chaplin. I felt like a man and it felt good.

When I got back to the flat at about 11.30, Mum and Dad were just going to bed. 'Have a good night?' Dad asked.

'Brilliant,' I replied and went to bed. I couldn't sleep, the night's events rolling through my mind, snapshots of the encounter bouncing in my head. Carol, fifteen and just out of school, was a pretty and petite brunette with a sunshine smile and sparkly green eyes. I was smitten.

The next day, Saturday, I woke up early, Dad and Mum were getting ready for work. 'Morning,' I said with a smile, and with a deep breath broke the news. 'I've got a girlfriend. She's really nice, can she come with us tonight?'

'Really?' Mum said. 'That'll be all right, won't it, Alb?'

'OK by me,' Dad replied, picking up his crash helmet and heading for the docks.

Just recently the band and I had been playing weekends in a pub in Bermondsey, and I'd mentioned this to Carol. She said she would like to come and watch, so the next job was to go round and ask her to come. I spruced myself up a bit. I think I was wearing pink jeans – those were the days – and started the walk across the estate to Carol's house. I must say I was a little nervous. Perhaps we didn't have an ongoing relationship, perhaps for her it was just a one-night thing, perhaps she had a boyfriend. I got to the house and knocked on the door. It was opened by Carol's younger brother.

'Is Carol there, please?' I said.

'Carol!' he shouted. 'Someone for you.' I didn't really like the 'someone', I think I would have preferred 'knight in shining armour' or something.

Carol appeared, looking lovely, and smacked a big reassuring kiss on my lips. 'Come in,' she said. 'Come and meet my mum and dad.' I had already learned in life that without a smattering of pain there was usually no gain, so I was ready. In I went and with my best handshake and my best butter wouldn't melt in my mouth look, made their acquaintance. They seemed nice people. Mum was pretty glamorous and seemed to call the shots, and Dad had a moustache and a quiet manner. The brother, Stephen, was a typical younger brother, still at the age when you think girl-friends and kissing are seriously unhygienic and seriously soppy.

We attempted conversation over a cup of tea. They asked a few questions, I gave a few answers, then asked if their pride and joy could accompany me to darkest Bermondsey to see the band that night. After a couple of reassurances they agreed.

At the end of what would be the first of many visits to Carol's house that afternoon, with everything fresh, new and exciting between us, I left around five to pack up my drums for the gig, leaving my new girlfriend in a state of anxiety about meeting my mum and dad. I reassured her with one last kiss and told her we'd pick her up at seven.

'I'll be ready,' she replied.

'They'll really like you,' I said. 'I do.'

'I really like you,' she replied and with a last wave off, I went to dismember my hi-hat.

We picked Carol up at seven, and with Dad's Ford Popular bulging with young lovers, Mum, Dad and a Slingerland drum kit, we headed for the bright lights of Bermondsey.

The Everons seemed to go down pretty well in this pub as long as we never played anything resembling blues. At various times I had persuaded the band to attempt it, but a word in the ear from our paymaster and burly publican meant we had to make a concerted effort to 'keep it lively'.

The clientele entered into the occasion clapping, dancing and generally applauding my drum solo in 'Wipe Out', except for two old boys who would shout 'Turn it down' from time to time. As we ran through our repertoire my thoughts were obviously on Carol and how she was doing with her 'new in-laws'. No worries, she was up and dancing with my mum, and obviously enjoying herself. Mum loves to dance and still goes line dancing today.

Well, life settled into a new and oldish pattern: work Monday to Friday on the factory shop floor, band practice, gigs, and time with Carol. As time passed we discovered all the things young couples discover, although I found some of our escapades some-what nerve-racking as emotions rose in the hall, with only the width of a council house door between us and Carol's mum and dad.

It was about this time, with money in my pocket and the driving ban for borrowing Dad's motorbike lifted, that I started to think of getting a scooter.

If you were a Mod you basically had two choices – a Lambretta or a Vespa. It was bit tricky for me, for although I dressed as a Mod I think deep down inside I was really a Rocker. I certainly preferred motorbikes and wasn't particularly in love with the inherent vanity of the Mod culture, being fundamentally a scruff. Anyway a man at work said he had a Lambretta TV for sale and it seemed to be the answer. In retrospect, it certainly wasn't. The bloody thing broke down in an image-shattering way on Bank Holiday runs to Brighton and Clacton, leaving me to run the risk of being pummelled by passing Rockers in sad lay-bys. I'm sure I pushed the thing further than I rode it. Thanks, mate!

East End Mods used to strip down their scooters, taking off the panels and other superficial bits. Not for us the chrome bubbles, we were minimalist. We would wear parkas and small berets on our bonce, not a foxtail in sight. This suited me as hardly any-thing stayed on my scooter, most of it fell off. I fell off once or twice too. The most dramatic occasion was when a car signalled right, so I though I'd pass on the inside. Instead it turned left and

I had to make a hasty detour, straight into Leytonstone Station car park – sideways!

I spent the last six months of my sixteenth year wishing for a car. Life in the factory was becoming tedious, so I was looking forward to my annual holiday.

Brian and Sandra's dad, Ted, was a big help with the band's bookings and had organized a playing holiday in Cattolica. The plan was to fly on a package holiday to Italy, attend an audition with a club and hopefully secure a booking. The Everons were poised to go international!

This was mega for me, my first time abroad and my first time in an aeroplane. I'm still not sure how those things stay in the air, even though I qualified for a private helicopter pilot's licence a few years later. Yes – Captain Cook.

So, pretty excited, Mum, Dad and I started to think about packing. It was their first time abroad too, so Mum was making serious inquiries with more travelled folk – you know, people who had been to France or even the Isle of Man – to see if they had essentials in far away Italy, like tea bags, milk and soap.

We were due to fly out on Saturday morning, so after work on Friday I made my way round to Carol's for what would be our last evening together for a couple of weeks. We had a good time, I think we sat outside a pub with a Babycham and a pint of brown and mild. She was sad that I was going away. To be honest, my sadness was tempered by the prospect of the following day's journey into the unknown.

The next morning we all met and made our way to the airport. Brian, John and Sandra carried their guitars. I had packed drumsticks and Mum had a treasure trove of tea bags. The flight was brilliant and we soon landed in Italy. The first thing that hit me was the smell. It smelt foreign, warm and musty, and a prevailing whiff of coffee filled the balmy air. I liked the semi-decayed feel of the buildings, and I still do. Today, most of Europe looks similar, but back in the Sixties it looked very different from England, and I found it fascinating.

To a boy used to council flats the package hotel was like the Ritz. Our rooms even had two toilets, although Brian's dad, who had been to Italy before, said that one was called a bidet – I've no idea how you spell it, but apparently Arabs used it instead of toilet paper he informed us.

The group settled in and started to enjoy themselves. Brian and I would cut loose in Cattolica while the rest would spend time at a very packed beach. Dad was constantly annoyed at having to pay for beach beds and umbrellas, it was the kind of rip-off they could never get away with in Clacton, he insisted.

Brian and I seemed to cause quite a stir in our English fashions. The Beatles, Swinging London and all that was English was revered world-wide at that time. (After all in a couple of years England would cement its place in history by winning the World Cup, thanks to three West Ham players!) England was the centre of the Universe, which explained why the local signorinas were paying us more than a passing interest. Brian loved it, but I of course had a steady girlfriend, plus I've never been good at detecting female interest unless it was really obvious – when it was my instinct to back away.

One afternoon, though, I was buying an ice cream in a bar. I was served by a very pretty dark-eyed girl. She spoke no English, and my Italian was a non starter, but something happened. I've had moments like that since, when a look can cut right through any language barrier and the fact that you're from different parts of the world adds to the intrigue. I held out my hand full of money. As the girl counted out the required amount in Italian and smiled, I smiled back.

'David,' I said, trying to make it sound as Italian as possible.

'Margarita,' she replied, sounding very Italian, and with one last smile I wandered off with my gelati.

Arrangements had been made for the audition at a club in town that afternoon at four, so we all met in the hotel reception and made our way to the club in good time.

The club was like a giant circus tent with a large stage at one end littered with bits and pieces belonging to the resident band and, luckily, a drum set. We met the genial manager and set up as best we could with the borrowed equipment. Brian's tuning-up sessions were endless, and sometimes half-way through a song he'd stop and tune up. At last we were set and blasted off with the song 'Money', one of our strongest, followed by 'Twist and Shout', another big tune. We got the job. Brian's dad did the negotiations, and millions were involved, unfortunately they were Lire.

We were engaged to play for forty-five minutes, after a magician's set and before the resident band's last set, which meant going on about ten o'clock.

The group were really pleased, there was talk of 'If we make it in Italy we could live here' and 'Perhaps we should learn Italian?' All this and we hadn't even made our debut.

That evening, as we manoeuvred around the hotel buffet, I started to think of Margarita and wondered if she would like to witness our conquest of Italy. So after dinner, I shook off the rest of the group and walked to the bar where she worked. Of course Carol, back home, was in the back of my mind, but here I was in a new land with new experiences, and besides, we would be back together in ten days or so, and the fact that Margarita and I couldn't even understand each other presented an interesting challenge.

When I got to the bar Margarita was frothing up a cappuccino. There was a smile of recognition as I walked in and sat down. I ordered a Pepsi from the waiter, and found a seat, catching her eye as she went about serving. I sat and puzzled over how to make coherent contact. After about three more caffeine-laden fizzy drinks I decided to make an attempt.

'Do you like music?' I asked.

'Si mucha,' she replied with a smile. So far so good. I then tried to tell her that I was in a band that was playing in a local club and to ask her if she would like to come and see us. All of which was greeted with confused looks and nearly a cheese sandwich. It was at this awkward moment that a waiter who spoke some English stepped in; he also turned out to be her older brother. Acting as a reluctant interpreter, he translated. I'm not sure how much truth was being relayed to each party, but it seemed Margarita was not allowed to go to clubs and not allowed to miss a night's work. A pregnant pause ensued as two tutti frutti ice creams were purchased by a very fat German. I finished off the dregs of a drink I didn't even want, and as older brother passed by with some empties, I went for the last throw of the dice.

'Would Margarita like to come out with me one night?' I honestly wasn't confident. I not only had to seek approval from Margarita but the brother as well. Who knew what he was actually saying to her? After a long discussion and various glances my way, I was beginning to wish I'd never entered this awkward love triangle. Big Brother came over – she could meet me there after work about 11.30 the next day.

'Fine,' I replied. 'Thank you.'

He carried on – 'I come to. Chaperone.'

'Right,' I enthused, and with a 'See you tomorrow' to both my dates, I made my way back to the hotel.

In bed I was trying to come to terms with this bodyguard concept. Maybe it was an Italian thing, and it was sensible, I had to admit. After all, they didn't know me. I could carry her off in my drum case back to England and the family would lose a willing helper.

My relationship with Carol seemed so much easier, and I missed her a lot that night.

The next morning at breakfast I circumnavigated the 'Where

48

were you last night?' questions and steered conversation to the show, and which set list we should play. We came to an agreement that we should play a fair whack of Beatles and Chuck Berry tunes, up-tempo and friendly stuff, and not chance any of the wrist-slashing blues repertoire I had instigated. After all, folks were there for a jolly-up, not a depressed wallow.

We spent most of the day on the beach, Dad still smarting from the price of a rented umbrella and me playing football with the locals, some of whom had christened me Georgie Best, not because of the skill factor, I fear, more because of the haircut.

Dinner time was looming, so with lobster red noses and very red shoulders we made our way back to base.

I don't like to eat much before a show, so I picked my way through a light meal and thought of the show and the scheduled, rather strange meeting with Margarita and her brother later. I left the group and went upstairs to get ready for a nine o'clock meet in reception and a taxi to the 'gig' – as dear old Reg would call it.

I took a shower and donned jeans, shirt and a collarless jacket, and with a splash of Old Spice I was ready.

When we got to the club it was busy, a good mix of holiday-makers and locals sat semi-enthralled watching the magician do his magic. He was down on the dance floor bit, so we were able to get up on the stage and fumble about in the darkness, plugging in and preparing to start when the magical one finished.

We were told his final trick was a plate-spinning thing and to be ready to go when the compère introduced us. At last the plates were spinning, aided by his slightly over-weight assistant in glittering tutu, and the big finish came with not a plate broken.

'Ladees and gentlemen – all the way from Engerland – The Everons!'

The lights went up, Johnny counted us in and we launched into 'Johnny Be Good'. The reaction was immediate, if maybe mixed. Some people hit the dance floor, some rocked in their seats, some ignored us and some sat with fingers in their ears and a pained expression. Mid-way through the second chorus I got a tap on the shoulder from the compère.

'It's too loud.'

'What?' I replied, kind of proving his point.

'Turn it down,' he shouted. I gave a sympathetic nod. We turned down, except for me of course, as there ain't no volume knob on a drum set and I certainly wasn't going back to brushes.

Slowly, most fingers came out of most ears and a good time was had by all. The reaction was very good on the whole and our new employers seemed happy. I don't think we conquered Italy, but we certainly secured a job for the holiday.

Time was ticking by, so I left the group buzzing in an after-show high and made my way to my rendezvous at Margarita's bar. When I got there, they were cashing up and bringing in the outside tables and chairs for the night. I gave Big Brother a hand and he asked how the show went.

'They seemed to like it,' I said.

With all the packing and cashing done and after a free drink, we seemed ready to roll. Now I wasn't at all sure how this 'three-some' deal was meant to go down. Did the chaperone stand in the middle? Did I ask him first if I wanted a kiss? I mean what was it all about? Did we all hold hands? I had no idea.

We decided to take a walk on the beach. To my relief, Big Brother found a seat and policed the proceedings from a reason-able distance. Margarita was a shy and pretty girl and her attempts at English were cute. My attempts at Italian were ridicu-lous. You know the kind of thing – speaking English slowly and loudly and putting the odd 'o' at the end of words in the hope of them sounding Italian. Given this slight drawback we got on well and, at a safe distance from her minder, we held hands. It was exciting for both of us, and the fact that we couldn't communicate through language seemed to add to the mystique. The night was warm and starry, and all in all the 'threesome' thing was not as awkward as I feared.

After a while we walked back to Margarita's brother, who was kind of keeping an eye on us but pretending not to, and the three of us went back to pick up his car by the bar. With a kiss on the cheek for Margarita and a shake of the hand for Big Brother, arrangements were made to see each other the following day and they drove off with a wave and a smile into the night.

As I walked back to my hotel I thought how romantic and old-worldly the encounter had been. Even though little contact had been made, it was quite an erotic experience, and thoughts of my Italian girlfriend and the show filled my mind as I wandered the empty streets of Cattolica, feeling a bit like a secret agent and pretty grown-up.

The rest of our working holiday played out. By the third night Margarita's brother obviously felt that I could be trusted and gave up his chaperone job. The days were fun and the shows at the club were well received. It had been a really good trip, but now it was time to go back to Blighty.

On our last night Margarita and I had exchanged kisses and addresses, but the time had come to pack the memories and clothes and head for home. On the plane I started to think about Carol, and although things had been a little rocky between us before I left, I was looking forward to seeing her.

We all made it back safely, and the band and I made arrangements to rehearse the next week and try to move the band forward, make a record or something, or really work for some kind of breakthrough.

Mum, Dad and I arrived home, much to the relief of Mum – at last a proper cup of tea! We unpacked and I decided to go round to Carol's. I felt a little guilty about my 'holiday romance', even though I'd told Margarita I had a girlfriend at home. I'm not sure she understood. I think she thought I meant a sister, and

I wasn't really prepared to go into detail.

I got to Carol's front door and knocked, the door opened and there stood Carol. I took a sharp intake of breath – Carol was blonde!

'Do you like it?' she said.

'Yes,' I managed. 'I think so.' I think the problem was that it didn't look blonde so much as yellow. I didn't like it, but when someone has done something that they think you will like and you don't, it's tricky. Instead of putting a downer on proceedings, I decided to give this dramatic change of hair colour some time, in the hope it would grow on me, or maybe grow out.

The traveller had returned, and Carol and her family were eager to hear all the ins and outs of the 'Italian job'. I obliged, leaving the Margarita bit on hold for another time. I did intend to tell Carol, as we had been on and off in recent weeks, but for the moment the hair was taking up a lot of my attention.

I still though a lot of Carol. After all, she was my first girlfriend and we had spent some good times and learned many things together, but I'm sad to say the hair change looked to me like another nail in the coffin of our relationship. What made it worse was that she had changed it for me. In a humdrum moment before going away, I had said, 'Why not dye your hair blonde?' Blonde would have been OK, but yellow was not so good. I did my best to be friendly, but something had gone between us, mainly I suppose the black hair.

We were still going out with each other, but the gaps between visits gently started to open. Carol had got a job at the same factory as me, which made our not talking to each other episodes at times difficult, and, sadly, the relationship finally ended when I found her in a more than friendly situation with another apprentice on the factory roof. The end had come, but she will always have a special place in my heart.

Occasional letters from Margarita would arrive, written with the aid of an Italian/English dictionary, and although I'm sure she did her best they were not easy to decipher. I was lucky to understand half the content, and I think that after a respectable time we both realized it would be difficult to develop a real relationship between us. It was probably easier to communicate with the brother, but sadly he was not my cup of tea. As the months went by the letters tailed off.

Footloose and fancy free again, most of my thoughts were now on becoming a professional musician, and it was around this time that a meeting that would change my life took place.

# 4

# The Meeting of the Mentor

In the middle 1960s, businessmen who knew little about music saw there was money in them there bands, and such was the case with Brian's employer, a kindly cooper called Stan Murray. Brian, between throwing barrels around, had mentioned the band to Stan, who had a daughter or son or something in a chart-making group of the time called the Honeycombs. Now, for the good of the group, Brian made an approach to him about his managing us.

Stan, to his credit, admitted he didn't know much about 'pop groups', but he knew a show business journalist and critic who might, a man called Derek Bowman. Brian made arrangements for Stan and Derek to come and watch us in rehearsal above a pub in Stratford called The Eagle.

I'll never forget that Wednesday night. The two of them turned up at the agreed time of eight o'clock, looking a little out of place in an East End pub, although they were both dressed so immaculately they could have been gangsters.

They introduced themselves and bought us drinks. Derek looked a little like a Brian Epstein figure in a grey Mohair suit and, smoking Peter Stuyvesant fags, he looked cool. Stan, who was dressed in a fawn-coloured crombie and wore a lot of jewellery, was a small round man with wavy grey hair and a friendly smile, a little like Sid James. We talked nervously for a while, then invited our would-be managers upstairs to have a listen.

By this time, I had started to write songs. No one in the group had before, but I thought it was important to try and develop our own style and identity rather than just doing covers of other people's tunes. Ironically the first song I ever wrote was called 'Carol-Anne' after you know who – 'Oh Carol-Anne, the day that you leave me, girl, I'll be a dying man.' Well she'd left and I wasn't, so it just goes to show you can't believe everything you hear in a lyric.

For the audition we had decided to do a mix of covers and songs that I'd written. The rehearsal room was a small hall that smelt of beer. We had set up at one end and put out a table and chairs for Derek and Stan. I don't know why but I was incredibly nervous. Something in the back of my mind told me that this was a pivotal, perhaps crucial meeting. John made a little speech and we launched into a Memphis Slim number. Stan looked a little overwhelmed by the volume, while Derek watched intently. By about the third number the nerves and edginess had gone and some of us were even starting to smile. Not Sandra, she never smiled, but I kind of liked that.

After the showcase we ordered some drinks and waited for the verdict. They liked us and agreed to manage us. Stan would be the Money Man, because he had money, and Derek would be the Ideas Man, because he had experience of showbiz.

When the gents left we were ecstatic. We were on our way. At last we had contacts and someone to guide us and, to some extent, believe in us. We congratulated Brian for making the approach and each other for simply being wonderful.

Over the next weeks things started to move on. Derek and Stan would attend the rehearsal periods at The Eagle, and Derek would bring down various showbiz people to promote word-of-mouth excitement around the group. It's amazing to think of the people he was able to drag down to the East End. People like Peter O'Toole, Lionel Bart, Ian McShane, Mary Quant, Susan Hampshire, Vidal Sassoon and many others came to see the group that Derek had discovered. Everybody who came seemed to like what they saw and heard, and we received a tremendous amount of encouragement from all and sundry.

One night at one of our regular band meetings Derek voiced an opinion that he thought a change of name for the band would be a good idea. He wasn't too fond of the Everons, and felt it would be a good idea to find a name that was more East End. He also had this fixation about doing an instrumental version of Limehouse Blues, all I suppose to give the band a bit more identity. For our name he had the idea of using Cockney rhyming slang, and we listened as usual in a positive way as Derek suggested 'China Plates' – rhyming slang for mates. The reaction was not exactly ecstatic, but Derek was our man. We believed in him and he believed in us, so China Plates we became.

Derek's next move was to spend a bit of Stan's dosh on matching clothes for the band, which entailed a trip to Carnaby Street for trendy fab gear. Of course, we had a girl in the band, so a perfect match wasn't on the cards, but we were decked out in white tab collar shirts, sky blue jackets, black strides and some rather dashing boots with Cuban heels, while Sandra did her best with a female version.

Next, a recording session was arranged in a flea-pit studio in Leytonstone. The plan was to record a demo that Derek could shop around to record companies.

We decided to record three tracks, two that I had written – 'Got to Work' and 'Carol-Anne' – plus a Memphis Slim song.

The prospect of actually hearing what we sounded like was both worrying and exciting as we set up under the guidance of the studio owner and engineer, a fat, bearded man who clearly hadn't seen the outside world for years. Headphones, vocal booths

*Above:* Mum, aged 14, hopping down in Kent with her cousin Albert, who was brought up in a Dr Barnardo's home, and his lady friend Myfanwy. I don't know who the boy is, I think he just wanted to be in the picture.

*Right:* Dad looks on as I meet Santa for the first time. Santa asked me what I wanted for Christmas. I told him a big gold torch!

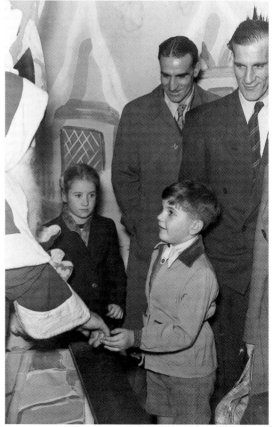

*Above:* In the playground in Canning Town where we played football, cricket and everything. Sometimes we even played war games, but nobody ever wanted to be the Germans. That's Blacky in the middle.
*Below:* Me and my cultured left foot. That's our flat.

*Top:* My first professional photo from a photo session shot on the Embankment in London in the Sixties.
*Above:* My first R & B band The China Plates. Brian, me, Sandra and John pictured at our weekend residency at the Bell pub in Ilford, around 1964.

*Left: Godspell* at the Roundhouse - and they never dropped me once. Such was the effect of the show that, as I was carried through the audience after the simple crucifix- ion, I would hear the audience sobbing. *Below:* Working with Ringo Starr in *That'll Be The Day* was nearly too much fun. Here we are on location at a crazy golf course in the Isle of Wight.

*Opposite page top:* Baby Verity, me and Maureen on the Isle of Wight, filming *That'll Be The Day*. A couple of days after this photo was taken Verity started to walk. *Below:* Jeff Wayne and I run through the song *On And On* at our first recording session at Advision Studios, 1972.

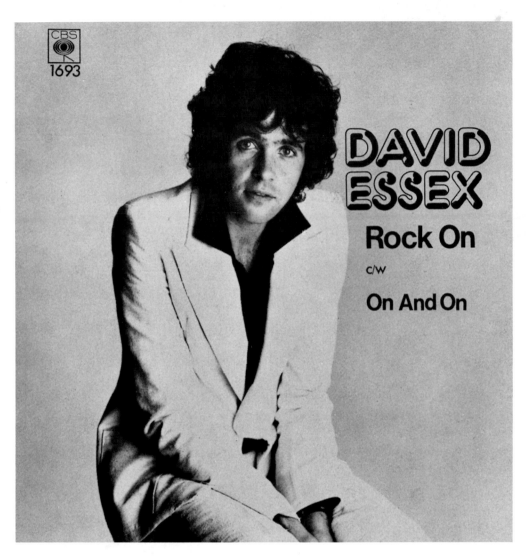

*Opposite* Recording *Rock On*. This picture was taken as I sang the actual take that appeared on the record.
*Above:* David Bailey's photo for the cover of what became my first worldwide hit – *Rock On*.

After the signing we managed to get out using dustbin lids as shields.

Derek, my manager, surveys the mayhem at another record signing for
*Rock On* at HMV on Oxford Street.

and many other gadgets were alien to us as we had never been inside a recording studio, let alone made a record, and for the first few takes various China Plates froze, making mistakes in songs we had played a thousand times.

The toughest part for me was that I was used to singing and playing the drums, but here we were laying down the backing track first, with vocals to be added later. This meant that sometimes, without the guidance of a vocal, people would lose their place. Also the balance in the 'cans' was really strange, and it sounded like we were playing somewhere a long way away, like Cattolica.

Finally we mastered this new environment and went into the control room to hear ourselves back. I think we were relieved. It sounded pretty good. Derek seemed pleased, the bearded studio man was complimentary, and we had made our first recording.

After this brush with recording I began thinking of realizing my ambition to become a professional musician. I was now just seventeen, in a decent group which had decent managers and we even had matching outfits. The trouble was, I had signed a contract for five years as an apprentice electrical engineer, and obviously to become professional I would have to ask for a release. I decided to talk things over with Derek first, and then of course with Mum and Dad.

I met up with Derek at the Arts Theatre Club in London's West End and told him I was thinking of turning pro. He presented a balanced argument as he always did, reassuring me of the talent he thought I had but also pointing out that success in the pop world was like winning the pools and not many people did that. We decided I should talk things over with my parents before making a decision, but to be honest my decision was already made.

Mum and Dad voiced responsible arguments about security and 'a trade to fall back on', but as always they wanted me to be happy. After some deliberation I decided to meet with Mr Baker, the personnel manager, and ask for a release.

I was nervous as I waited outside his office. What if he said no? Would that mean four more years in the factory? I'd be twenty-one, ancient, by the time I was allowed to leave. Would I be past my rock'n'roll prime?

'Come in, Cook,' Mr Baker called, and in I went to meet the man who could decide my destiny.

I explained that I felt I was not totally gripped by my present vocation and really my wish was to be a musician, which meant, I suppose, tearing up the contract.

Mr Baker sat back and took another puff of his pipe. It was getting a bit difficult to see the whites of his eyes through the clouds of smoke, but I was hopeful.

'Well, son,' he said at last, 'if you feel you want to leave there's not much point in staying, is there?' He wished me well and said if things didn't work out the door was always open. It was a top response from a good man. I wonder if he knew in later years that apprentice Cook turned into David Essex and in a way he set me free to follow a dream.

Derek meanwhile had approached a few record companies without much success. The China Plates, although now professional, were barely ticking over. Our matching outfits were hanging under-used in wardrobes and Stan was becoming disillusioned with his investment. There was a crisis brewing.

Derek called me and asked if we could meet. We met again at the Arts Theatre Club, where he explained that Stan had finally lost interest, which I think we as a group had already suspected. But what was to come next was a big surprise. Derek went on to explain that the main reason he became our manager was because of the potential he said he recognized in me, and that the many people he had brought to see us singled me out as something special. I was flattered, but what did this mean?

He then asked, 'Would you like to be a solo singer?' Now this was a long way from my ambition of being a jazz drummer and something I had never ever thought of doing. After all, I had only sung under orders from John and Brian. It seemed that Derek too had misgivings about the Chinas' future but believed I could make it, but did I want to?

I've always been a very loyal person, so to walk out on the group on a personal mission wasn't my style. 'I don't know' was my noncommittal answer. We parted and I had much to think about. I walked through the West End, and a strange sadness came over me. I remembered the happiness we felt as a band, united as we conquered Italy, how we were convinced that it was only a matter of time, now that we had managers, shopping in Carnaby Street full of hope and optimism. I wondered what had happened. We were still the band that only months ago proper showbiz people were enthusiastic about, convincing us of our bright future to come. Now, it seemed, we had no future.

By the time the group met for another seemingly pointless rehearsal the mood was one of doom and gloom. All members had had calls from Derek regarding Stan's withdrawal and had been informed that Derek couldn't carry on and finance the venture on his own.

Not much music was played that night, and John even talked of breaking the group up. This surprised me, as I was committed to making it work, and this lack of belief in the band's future from the band itself started to fuel my thoughts regarding Derek's solo singer thing. Brian's belief in the group was total, but John and Sandra seemed resigned to failure, and I was set on making my life in music.

Days and weeks went by, and slowly but surely the band's momentum waned until one day I decided to believe in Derek's belief in me and left the band.

I haven't seen the band since. I think John and Sandra married and moved to Australia, I'm not sure where Brian is, but I hope they are happy and well and managed to sell the group's Bedford Dormobile before it finally fell to bits.

I rang Derek and told him that if he was serious about me going 'solo', then I was too.

# 5

# Coming Out from Behind the Cymbals

Now that I'd left the group, Derek, carrying a contract under his arm, came over to meet with me and my parents to talk about the future. We talked for a long time and the belief that dear Derek had in me was very clear, far stronger than my own belief. Derek was fast becoming part of the family and we all respected him.

I started to learn more about the man. Derek was an academic, with a Bachelor of Arts degree from Oxford. He spoke eight languages (where was he when I met Margarita?). He also had an amazing knowledge of theatre and film and, as I said before, a belief in me that was unshakeable. Derek was tall, dark and good-looking, about fifteen years or so older than me – the older brother I never had.

After a few hours Derek left, leaving the contract with my parents to look over and sign on my behalf. Mum, Dad and I discussed my uncertain future far into the night. They were understandably concerned: I'd left my job, I'd left the group, I'd left my girlfriend, and now due to Derek's influence, I was to become a solo singer, something I had never thought of being. I didn't even really like singing. Clearly a little more time was needed to ponder the possibilities, so the Cooks hit the sack.

The next morning no one spoke of our dance with destiny. Dad and Mum went to work as usual, and not one of us men-

tioned the tricky decisions regarding my future. It was as if we all
knew we needed more time. Later that morning, as I was listening
to a blues album, instead of listening primarily to the drums, as I
had in the past, I focused on the singers, and something remarkable happened. A song featuring Buddy Guy hit me. I was so
taken by the emotion in his voice that there and then I decided to
be a singer. If Buddy Guy could move me and communicate so
much with his voice and performance, what a wonderful thing it
would be for me to try and do. It was then that I started to take
this singing lark seriously.

At tea that night I told Mum and Dad that I did want to sing,
and was committed to going it alone and was confident with
Derek by my side. To their eternal credit they agreed to sign
Derek's contract and the quest began.

Looking back I realize how concerned Mum and Dad must
have been. There was no history of musicians or showbiz, let
alone pop stars in the family. It must have been mysterious and
worrying to gamble their son's future in an unknown world, but
just as with the drums in the council flat they gave me the
opportunity. It's something I've tried to do with my own children.

Derek was really pleased with our decision and soon set about
devising schemes to teach this raw talent the skills of the craft. To
me, a few of the plans seemed a very long way from Buddy Guy.

The first place he sent me to was a church hall in Marleybone,
where a wonderful elderly black American called Buddy Bradley
gave tap dancing lessons – yeah, tap dancing lessons. I went two
evenings a week and learned to tap dance. I think the drums and
my sense of rhythm must have helped, because Buddy reckoned I
was a natural. I really liked Buddy, but wasn't too convinced that
I would tap dance my way to the stars.

Then came singing lessons. These took place in a rehearsal
room in Soho with a learned old fellow named Eric Gilder. Eric
looked like a wise old owl and forced out of me renditions of light

opera and standards. I believe this was useful, as it gave me the confidence to sing in front of somebody without hiding behind the cymbals and taught me a lot about voice production and breath control.

Derek would attend the dancing and singing lessons, willing his prodigy on, marvelling at the progress. I was starting to feel more like Sammy Davis Jr than Buddy Guy.

Next he started on the acting. Derek sent me to see Robin Ray, an acting and voice coach. We acted speeches and looked at vowel sounds. I think this was when my West Ham accent began to soften. I was even enrolled on a two-week course at RADA (The Royal Academy of Dramatic Art), where I was given a Shakespearean speech to deliver. It might just as well have been in Chinese – remember me, the footballer?

In retrospect, although all these things seemed a bit straight to me at the time, I'm sure they taught me much and have been of use over the years.

With some of the rough edges knocked off, Derek was now looking for work and experience for me. I was broke, and Derek would bung me a fiver now and again to keep me going, but both of us needed some money coming in.

I would pop out some nights to a club to see a band, and once every two weeks or so I would accompany Derek to the theatre where he would review plays. As a critic, he was sent first or second night tickets to review and publicize productions.

I'll never forget the first time I went to the theatre. I was mesmerized, not only by the actors and the play, which by the way was Sean O'Casey's *Juno and the Paycock*, but by how civilized the audience were. I was used to beer bottles whizzing past my head, indifference to the music we were playing, and drunks falling over my cymbals. This was so polite, almost reverential. The audience were attentive and enthusiastic. It was probably then that I first thought how good it would be to work in the theatre.

Around this time Derek had applied for David Cook to join Equity (the actor's union), but there was already a member called David Cook, so we had to think of a new name. It was important for me to join – no union meant no work. Derek rang me and suggested David Essex, as I was now living in Essex, I wasn't too sure, but as usual I went along with it, and now I'm just glad I wasn't living in Middlesex!

Although Derek was educating me in the art of showbiz, my heart lay and still lies in music. Derek had been busy on my behalf on the recording side and had found some interest from a wonderful man called Bunny Lewis.

Bunny was an independent producer who released records through the Philips Fontana record label, so a meeting was set up and off we both went to a flat in Knightsbridge. When I first met Bunny he certainly wasn't what I thought a record producer would be like. Bunny was a middle-aged man, very English with sticky-out teeth – hence, I suppose, the nickname. We stood around a piano and an arranger taught me a song that Bunny had found, a big Walker Brothers-type ballad called 'And the Tears Came Tumbling Down', written by Perry Ford of the group called The Ivy League. Bunny had this vision of a boy crying while performing the song. I thought – no chance.

But I learned the song and gave Bunny an earful. Dear Bunny seemed to like what he heard, presented us with a recording contract and a date in the studio. Derek and I could hardly contain ourselves as we almost danced our way down Knightsbridge. This was it – next stop the charts.

When the day of the recording session arrived I was both excited and scared. My throat felt funny, and I wasn't sure if I knew the song, although I'd practised it at home a thousand times – even Mum and Dad knew it inside out. The nerves were killing. I still get nervous when performing, but have learned, as all performers must, to use nerves in a positive way – not easy.

When I walked into the old Olympic Studios in Barnes, south-west London, and saw the orchestra I was speechless, never mind singless. There were musicians and musical instruments all over the place. A thirty-piece orchestra had been assembled for me to sing with, as well as backing singers. Bunny hopped down from the control room when he saw I'd arrived and, sensing the terror surrounding me, gently reassured me in his no-nonsense kind of way. Bunny was the kind of man who, if you were feeling unsure, would give you a kick up the backside rather than a reassuring whisper. Bunny's upper lip was definitely stiff.

The arranger, perched on the conductor's podium, brought the musicians to order, counted them in and told me to stand by him and listen to the run-through. I had never heard an orchestra live, and it sounded wonderful. I was amazed as I watched these ordinary-looking people produce such a magical sound, and my nervousness started to transform into a feeling of 'I want to be a part of this.' I felt very privileged that they were there and going to back me.

The recording commenced. I was in the vocal booth singing live as the orchestra went down, doing my best to convey Bunny's teary vision and stay in tune. After three takes Bunny was happy and we moved on to the B side. As the arranger went through the other song, I went to the control room to hear what we'd done. Bunny and Derek were listening intently. I didn't like the sound of my voice much and was surprised when Bunny shouted, 'Good. Good. I told you you could do it. Now go and do the other one – we lose the musicians in half an hour!'

We recorded the other song ('You Can't Stop Me From Loving You') quickly, just finishing before the deadline. In fact some of the musicians seemed to be packing up before the last note was played. In the days when the Musicians' Union was all powerful, the emphasis on time and money quite often got in the way of creativity.

With the two tracks recorded and the studio emptying, the tension started to ease. 'A cup of tea all round and we'll listen back,' said a happy Bunny. Tea was served and the engineer hit the playback button. I wasn't too pleased with my performance, but it did sound like a proper record. Buoyed by Bunny's enthusiasm, Derek and I left, leaving Bunny to mix the tracks.

It was April 1965 and the Beatles topped the charts with 'Ticket to Ride'. We meanwhile eagerly awaited our advance copies of my own chart hope. I remember the excitement when they arrived, all bearing that famous blue and silver Fontana label. I marvelled at the fact that my voice came out of those plastic grooves, and Mum and Dad looked proudly at the label.

Although I did some press interviews and a couple of Pirate Radio road shows, 'And the Tears Came Tumbling Down' sank without trace. It was played twice on Radio Luxembourg; I heard it once. I didn't know whether to run and hide or run into the street with my transistor radio shouting, 'Oi – that's me!'

All in all it was disappointing but Bunny was upbeat. Because of my blues background he'd found another song originally done by Solomon Burke called 'Can't Nobody Love You' – bad grammar but a good old blues song, something I could get my teeth into, and I did.

This record, released on 3 December 1965, did a little better than the first with regard to air play, and reached number seventeen in the Pirate Radio charts. To me this proved that you should stick to what you believe in, because somehow the Great British Public can sense honesty and belief in an artiste.

Around this time I started looking for a backing band, so I could get some work. I began to scan adverts in musical papers, and in the *Melody Maker* I saw an ad for a vocalist. I decided to call Pete, just as the ad instructed. Pete picked up the phone and with a voice like gargling with stones told me they were a rhythm and blues band called Mood Indigo, named after a Duke

Ellington classic. They were based in Stevenage and there were five of them. Pete had vaguely heard of me and we arranged to meet up in a couple of days at a band rehearsal in a warehouse in Hertfordshire.

The next day I thought I should let Derek in on my escapade. At first he was a little put out that I hadn't told him before calling Pete, but slowly he warmed to the idea.

So, with a lift from a friend called Frank, I made my way to an industrial estate in Stevenage on the agreed evening. Frank was a kind of Georgie Fame look-alike and we had some good times together. I remember one time when we rented a holiday chalet in Leysdown with some mates. It rained solidly all week. Frank decided to impress a girl with his souped-up Mini – well it did have black-and-white racing stripes on it. Frank went tearing round the campsite like Sterling Moss, only to skid through the front wall of our chalet, coming to rest under the kitchen sink where I was washing up. 'Cup of tea, Frank?' I asked. Frank was not amused.

When we found the rehearsal place there was a roaring rendition of the James Brown classic 'Night Train' filling the Hertfordshire air. It sounded good, and even Frank was impressed. I went into the warehouse, and Frank drove off to the local Chinese. This band had a fair amount of facial hair, they looked like musicians and sounded like musicians. There were two sax players, an organist, a bass player and a drummer. It was unusual not to have a guitarist, but it seemed to work.

We talked a while about the journey and the music we liked, then set about going through a couple of songs. 'Midnight Hour' seemed to be the popular choice and away we went. It felt good to have some power behind me; it was nice to be back in a band. The boys and I got on well both musically and sense of humour wise. I became their singer and they became my band.

Frank kindly picked me up and back we went. I was feeling

happy about being a member of a band again and sang along to Radio Caroline as we made our way home.

I told the folks the next day how good the band was and how I especially liked the black baritone sax player Paddy. Dad questioned the length of the journey to Stevenage. I could drive now, as I'd passed my driving test more or less as soon as my driving ban was lifted, and was using Dad's Ford Popular for transport – if and when I could borrow it. Of course I wanted my own car, and finally, with a little help from Dad, made moves to get one.

Mood Indigo were renting a van for gigs, so I thought if I bought a van, this would help with the costs. I'd have transport, and the band could pay a small sum to use it. The band liked the idea, so I bought a second-hand Ford Transit – a real babe magnet!

I remember one journey when we were driving along the North Circular and Pete exclaimed, 'Look at that tyre!' Seconds later the van dropped down on one side and skidded to a stop. It was our wheel that we had seen rolling along beside us. I was sent into a house to request our wheel back from this lady's front garden.

In my year or so with Mood Indigo we played rhythm and blues clubs up and down the country, including some of the places where I'd previously gone to watch bands, like The Flamingo, The Marquee and Eel Pie Island in the Thames, where you had to pay a penny toll to cross the bridge to the island.

There was so much live music then and so many bands, we would bump into regulars all playing the same circuit. There was Rod Stewart in Steampacket, for example, David Bowie, known then as Davey Jones and the Locker, and Elton John, who played keyboards for a band called Bluesology – there was respect between us and a little rivalry.

Probably the reason why the singers I mentioned still have followings today is that they have tremendous experience of playing live. I sometimes feel sorry for some of the new bands who only have experience of recording studio or video shoots and then are expected to tour, only succeeding in a shallow way, with dance routines and stage effects filling the void.

I had spent a good deal of time with the band, and now Derek was putting pressure on me to concentrate more on my solo career. I was having fun with the band, but we did seem stuck in a groove, and all that travelling just to rehearse had worn thin.

However, people were beginning to take notice. A comment in the *Record Mirror* was typical of the good reviews I was getting – 'a big voiced newcomer who punches lyrics like a heavyweight'.

With the near success of my return to black music with 'Can't Nobody Love You', Bunny decided to employ a heavyweight to produce my next record – J.J. Jackson. J.J. was maybe a pound or so lighter than Barry White but there was not much in it. A massive bejewelled black man, he had graduated from Detroit's famous Tamla Motown label and had even written a hit for himself in America called 'It's All Right'. I was thrilled at the prospect of working with him.

We routined a few classic rhythm and blues songs and J.J. decided we should record a Ray Charles song called 'This Little Girl of Mine', coupled with a song called 'Broken Hearted'. It was great to work with him. I thought 'This Little Girl of Mine' was a good record but although reviews were good – 'Tremendous talent,' said one, 'this young British blues-man and his performance of this top class Ray Charles number should click' – it didn't, so we took a step back.

With my life in recording limbo and the liaison with Mood Indigo running down, I had time on my hands and not much money. Frank had become manager of a club in Ilford called the El Grotto. I pulled up there one night to see Frank hitting an unwanted clubber with a portable bus stop – it was that kind of place.

One night, when Frank and I sat at the bar talking Bobby

69

Moore, West Ham and the meaning of life, two girls in very short skirts came in. Both were pretty but one was special. Our interest was short-lived, however, because then local playboy Phil the Greek came in and immediately joined them. Frank said he'd seen the girls before; one was called Kath and the one I liked was called Maureen. Suspecting they may have been part of Phil's harem, I asked Frank if Phil was going out with one of them. 'I don't think so,' replied Frank. Time ticked by and I decided to head for home, but as I went to walk out, to my surprise, Maureen gave me a wave. I waved back. Who could have known, at that point, what the future had in store for us both?

Having no real need for a van now, although in quieter moments I had used it to deliver carpets and other bits and pieces to help with the finances, I decided to buy a car.

The good thing about living in the East of London is there's no shortage of second-hand car dealers. I swapped the old faithful van for a Nash Metropolitan. As you may know, the Nash is a small American car from the late Fifties, most of them brought over at the time by American servicemen stationed in Britain. It was two-tone blue, with white-wall tyres, a bench seat and column gear-change – sweet as a nut, mate. Never been out in the dark, only one owner and she was a Nun. I did mile upon mile in it.

One night I decided to go and see a guitarist I knew. He was besotted by the Beach Boys but that night was playing a blues gig at the 100 Club in London's Oxford Street. I parked up, got to the club early and started talking to an elf-like tomboy who said her name was Beth, pronounced Bet. She was Swedish. Now, every eighteen-year-old boy is fully aware of the reputation Swedish girls have for free love. I don't know much about that, but Beth didn't look like your typical Swede. She had short brown hair and dressed a bit like a boy, no make-up and big boots.

Beth was an au pair for an American family in North London. Her father was a professor back in Upsala and she spoke perfect

English. After the ball was over I gave her a lift home back to an enormous house in a leafy road in Highgate. Beth and I spent nearly every evening together after that. She was great fun to be with, and a few tears were shed when after six months she had to return home to university in Sweden.

Work in showbiz had been patchy during the Beth period, and indeed before. Derek and I were waiting for something to click or for Bunny to resurface.

I did a few part-time jobs to help pay for the petrol to Highgate and dining out at Wimpy's. Window cleaning was one. I worked for a company that cleaned office buildings under contract. The foreman was a lovely man called Tommy, an old-fashioned Cockney with sparkly eyes, a thin moustache and a wicked sense of humour. Tommy led numerous determined visits to the local café. I've never seen people eat so much. Before work – a full breakfast, fried bread, the whole shebang. Eleven o'clock – cup of tea and a cake. One o'clock – big cooked lunch, meat, pud and afters. Four o'clock – tea and a bun, then off home for a massive dinner with the Mrs. Full working days like this were not that common, though. The boys had perfected a way of not cleaning the windows of the whole factory by isolating the office where the man who signed the work-completed docket worked. They would clean his windows beautifully and send me in to say, 'All done, Guvnor' and get our docket signed. In this way our daily work quota was usually over well before mid-day.

Other jaunts into the workplace consisted of painting factories – after a pint one lunchtime I fell out of a roof and ended up in hospital with concussion. There was a two-week stint in an hardware shop under a Hitler impersonator who was very unpleasant. There was also a week drilling holes in wooden things that held up tents, and peeling spuds in a fish and chip shop – so don't tell me I ain't seen life!

Undeterred, dear Bunny finally resurfaced and decided to persevere with J.J. I was pleased, as I had complete faith in him, although I must admit it was slightly shaken when he played me the song he had written for my next record. Called 'Thigh High', it was a tribute to the miniskirt. The chorus went 'Oh My Thigh High Dig Dem Dimples On Dem Knees.' Terrifying.

Giving the charismatic J.J. the benefit of the doubt, I dutifully went in and growled the thing in the manner he had dictated. It was a horrible record and probably rekindled my intent to write for myself. Needless to say the record never charted, and in retrospect I'm pleased it didn't. Who knows what other gems the liaison would have set loose upon the world?

The Bunny adventure had run its course. Bunny was down a few thousand pounds and with such a stinker of a record we had dented our credibility with the media. The *Daily Mirror* was right when it said, 'I've no complaints about the miniskirt but to put it in a song – Ugh!' It was time to end it.

Although things with Bunny had not worked out, I'm eternally grateful to the man for believing in me and giving me my first chance.

It seemed that with the downturn in fortunes, it was finally time to split from Mood Indigo. We had fun but it was difficult, mainly thanks to a mad booking agent who seemed to book us in Sunderland one night and Bournemouth the next. Eventually I came down with pneumonia in a very wet Manchester. We were going everywhere but, as far as my career was concerned, I was going nowhere. Romantically, my time on the road with the band had been interesting. There was a basic rule that if you got off with a girl for the night, you dipped into the band's communal fund for bed and breakfast; if not, you kipped in the van. I had formed a few liaisons but, being the shy one, was generally found sleeping in the van, usually with Pete.

I would miss the band and the laughs we had, but at least I wouldn't have to put up with Pete's snoring any more.

# 6

# Treading the Boards

Derek was now anxious to get me into theatre. He felt there was more justice there than in the pop world, where success, as he'd said before, was like winning the pools.

So, with a certain amount of trepidation, I dutifully attended an audition arranged by Derek for a touring repertory company. The company was run by an American called Zack Matalon and his wife Elizabeth Seale. Elizabeth was a successful musical performer and had made a mark in the musical *The Pyjama Game*. I'm not sure what Zack had been up to, but he was forming a touring company and I was auditioning for, I suppose, the juvenile lead roles.

Repertory theatre, on the decline these days, used to be a tremendous training ground for actors. I remember talking to the wonderful Frank Finlay when we did *Mutiny* together, who told me how useful rep was for him. Playing in one production while learning and rehearsing a part for the next week's production was certainly demanding, but obviously very good experience.

Zack's company was not quite a weekly repertory, but a company that would have four or five productions in its repertoire and tour with them. Derek was keen for me to gain valuable experience, so off I went to the audition and surprisingly got the job. I honestly didn't know what I was doing. I remember trying to look relaxed at the audition and making the mistake of going up-stage to lean on a piece of perspective scenery, a church steeple. It must have looked ridiculous, me, with my elbow resting on top of a church steeple, but it probably appealed to Zack's sense of anarchy. I of course was clueless – there was a bit of wood to lean on, so I leant on it.

Derek, Mum and Dad were really pleased and proud that I had landed my first job in the theatre. Rehearsal dates were set, a contract was signed and even though I was going to be paid peanuts, as most people still are in the theatre, I was looking forward very much to becoming a stage actor.

Soon the first day of rehearsals came around. The company were requested to meet in a church hall in Bayswater at ten a.m. I was really nervous on the tube from Newbury Park. I felt out of my depth and a long way from the drums and Buddy Guy, but knew I couldn't let Derek or my parents down. I made my mind up to do my best. When I found the hall it was around 10.15 and I could hear Zack's voice resonating through the closed doors. Sheepishly I opened them, and Zack stopped in his tracks.

'David,' he boomed. 'We wondered if you were coming.'

'Sorry, I couldn't find it,' came my meek reply.

'Let me introduce you,' said Zack.

To an East End boy introductions were pretty alien, but I did my best to be sophisticated. Derek had been doing some of this introduction stuff, so I'd had a little practice. First I met Roy, who was a classical actor type with a bald head and glasses and a loud and well-produced speaking voice. Then I met Susanne, a young actress who was posh, and miserable. By now names were going in one ear and out the other...There were two character actors who seemed friendly, a lady musical director, a ginger-haired girl who was the stage manager (I wasn't sure what that was, but she was dressed in black), a very white girl who looked like she lived under a toadstool, and a massive and impressive black man called Dambuza – that name went in.

Finding a chair, I joined the group and Zack outlined our future. We were going to rehearse three productions, a play, *To Dorothy a Son*, and two musicals, *Fantasticks* and *Oh Kay*. The stage manager, Ginger, handed out parts.

I was to play Mat the boy in *Fantasticks*, a Duke in *Oh Kay* and an off-stage phone voice in *To Dorothy a Son* – this especially appealed to me.

*Fantasticks* was the first one to tackle, so the musical director played and gave us a rendition of the songs we would be learning. She was a petite American girl in her thirties with glasses and a lot of hair. Although her performance lacked a little passion there were obviously some good tunes in the show, including 'Soon It's Gonna Rain' and 'Try to Remember' – a really nice score. John Michael Tebelak, the man who conceived *Godspell* – a show that would prove so important to me in the future – was very influenced by *Fantasticks*.

With the first day over, my nerves started to dissolve into anticipation. Later, on the Underground going east, I read the script and mentally acted my bits. You know how sometimes you see a slightly strange person muttering away to himself in a public place – well he's probably an actor learning his lines.

Over the next three weeks we polished our performances and sorted out digs for our opening week in Paignton, Devon. Zack's schedule was that once we were on and rolling we would address the other two productions, as we toured the country.

All this was brand new to me and I enjoyed it. I wasn't particularly nervous on the opening night, until I heard the audience applaud the overture...Blimey! The show seemed to be in slow motion – a bit like being in an accident. Your mind races and time slows down. It was good to get to the end and hear the reassuring response of the audience. Derek had travelled down for the opening and said some confidence-building things and gave me some useful notes. Much relieved, the cast and I enjoyed our first-night party and settled into life on the road.

As we travelled from one end-of-the-pier theatre to another, I would usually share a room with Dambuza. I liked him a lot. He was a Zulu who had fled South Africa in the time of apartheid, leaving with a show that came to the West End called *King Kong*, a musical based around a boxer he played.

We talked for hours. He earned my respect and admiration as he spoke about life in Africa, the struggle for freedom, and life in general. As for the rest of the cast, we all seemed to get along, there were occasional outbursts as we rehearsed and staged the other two shows, but nothing hysterical, except perhaps my performance as the Duke in *Oh Kay* – although the tap-dancing finally came in handy.

Relationships bloomed and faded in our tight-knit company. The musical director finally wore me down, I finally wore the ginger-haired girl down, and Zack tried his luck wherever he could.

It was just as Derek had predicted – good experience. While I'd been on the road and after the demise of Bunny Lewis, Derek had been talking to record producer Mike Leander. After a brief meeting between us, Mike suggested going into the studio to record a cover of a song on the new Beatles album *Sgt Pepper's Lonely Hearts Club Band* called 'She's Leaving Home'. I think what intrigued Derek was that it would be released only in the States, as the deal Mike had was with an American label called Uni, which was something to do with Universal Pictures.

I was game, so into IBC studios we went. Mike, unlike Bunny, looked from head to toe like a record producer. He wore an orange suit and had a foppish quality about him. A clever writer and arranger, Mike enjoyed much success before and after me. Recording with Mike was different from my previous experience of recording, as he was much more meticulous, and it was good experience to work with him.

We finished 'She's Leaving Home' and a song Mike had written for the B side called 'He's a Better Man Than Me', whereupon the masters were shipped to Hollywood for approval and were released in the spring of 1967.

When we recorded 'He's a Better Man Than Me' Mike wanted me to sing it with a very English accent, I suppose to give the Americans a taste of Swinging London. It was a truly magical time in the USA for all that was English, and when the record came out, US radio stations flipped it over. The result was a low chart entry in the US and a very surprised me. Puffed by this distant success, Mike approached me with another song, this time for release world-wide, which I think meant in Britain as well. This time he had a song by someone I like very much as a writer – Randy Newman.

It was a quirky little tune called 'Love Story', and was released in May 1968. For recording I was starting to use my voice in a different way, singing less like a Chicago-born blues singer with a bit of Tom Jones or Chris Farlowe thrown in, and making a smaller, more natural sound. The track was probably a little weird for the mainstream charts but it came out well and remains, I think, the only one of my recordings ever featured on the wacky – on purpose – John Peel radio programme. Nice to be cutting edge.

After 'Love Story' had restored a bit of credibility, Mike and I parted company. Mike didn't have the patience of Bunny.

Around this time a few little showcase appearances were arranged. Once I sang in a jazz club with the Dudley Moore Trio, and one tricky night I sang at the Kray brothers' club. After the show, which went very well, in front of a very nervous Derek, Ronnie asked if I wanted a manager.

'I've got one,' I replied.

'Is he any good?' Ron enquired.

'Yeah, great,' I reported.

Ronnie went on, 'If you need any help, son, you know where to come.'

'Thank you,' I said, and Derek said it was time to go.

A week later Derek called with news of an audition he thought I should go to for a Christmas show called *The Magic Carpet*. I went, did a rendition of a song that I did with Mood Indigo called 'Any Day Now', and secured the juvenile lead of Prince Zelim in a show bound for Guildford.

T'was now time to leave my humdrum life and return to the theatre. This mob was very theatrical: the writer was a very gay gentleman called John Dalby. I can't remember the director's name, but I know he gave me a hard time. It seemed this Prince didn't come from anywhere near Canning Town – he was very posh. 'Vowel sounds, David' was the cry from the director. I felt like Eliza Doolittle.

I spent most of my time acting with a thirty-foot dragon, and with a turban on my head, and for me the highlight was when the principal dancer, who must have crossed the boredom threshold that night, did his dance solo with a brown paper bag over his head.

On a night off, I went to see Frank at the club, and who should be there but Maureen and Kath. 'I'm sure they're lesbians,' Frank reported. 'You never see them dancing with blokes – only each other.' The girls came over to the bar next to me to buy a drink.

'Haven't seen you for ages,' Kath said.

'No, I'm working,' I said. 'Let me get you a drink.' Isn't it strange how, if you're talking to two girls, one of whom you fancy and the other you don't, you always find it easier to strike up a conversation with the one you don't fancy?...and so it went. Maureen was lovely, and the two of them should have been a comedy act as they were very funny. We met up a few times after that and slowly but surely an old-fashioned courtship started between Maureen and me.

With the recording career again in a state of disarray, Derek started to try to energize things on the theatre and even film front. This, as far as he was concerned, meant securing the services of an agent. We met with one of the most powerful showbiz legends, Leslie Grade. Les and his brothers, Lou and Bernard Delfont, practically controlled British show business at that time. Former variety performers themselves, they had built up an impressive empire encompassing variety, film and theatre, so to sign for them looked to be a good prospect.

A contract was signed and for ten percent Leslie would represent me. I liked Leslie, an elderly Jew from London's East End. With his expensive cigars and larger-than-life manner, he was exactly what you would think a theatrical agent would look like, and his direct energy was formidable.

I was sent almost immediately to attend an audition for understudy in an American musical called *Your Own Thing* that was scheduled to open at the Comedy Theatre in London in 1968. I got the job and enjoyed my time with it, making some good friends in the young American cast and going on a few times. Sadly the show closed before the English cast were due to take over.

A few film openings also happened around this time, largely thanks to Derek's efforts. I made a fleeting appearance in a film in which, coincidentally, Frank Finlay played the lead. I reminded him years later when we worked together on my own musical, *Mutiny*, of how kind and thoughtful he was to me on my film debut, whereupon he pleaded for patience regarding his singing ability as Captain Bligh. In fact Frank was wonderful in *Mutiny* and performed the score I'd written brilliantly. In the film we did together, which was called *Assault*, I played a motorbike rider who got blown up in a chemist's shop. Frank bought me a cup of tea in the canteen.

I remember a chilling moment in Los Angeles following

another bit part I did in a film called *All Coppers Are…* when two strange men came from behind a bush and said accusingly, 'We saw you in The Devil's Garden.' I thought my number was up, but all they wanted was my autograph. It turned out that the title *All Copper Are…* had been changed to *The Devil's Garden* for American consumption.

I also had a bit in a *Carry On* film, shot at Pinewood Studios. I must have been truly broke at the time, because I remember taking back some empty bottles to help with the petrol money to get there. The scene was classic *Carry On*, a worker's meeting in *Carry On Henry*. We were all decked out in Tudor dress as it was something to do with Henry the Eighth. The meeting was being addressed by Kenneth O'Connor, one of the principals, with whom I would also work again later. My job was to shout that immortal line 'What about the workers?' – which I did, rather convincingly I thought. It was to no avail, however, as the scene finished up on the cutting-room floor – probably a career let-off.

Meanwhile, back in my agent's office, Leslie Grade had put his son Michael in charge of my career. He was not a great agent, but he did sort out an audition for me to become a 'walking understudy' for Tommy Steele in the London Palladium's pantomime *Dick Whittington*. A walking understudy, I learned for the first time, doesn't take part in the show, but must be there in case the person they are understudying conks out. I got the job, which was good in one way, as it meant regular money for the seemingly endless three months that the production ran. It was also soul-destroying, however, having to check in every day for two shows a day just in case your services were called on. It's probably better to be in the show, even as a spear carrier, than sit around all afternoon and evening with nothing to do but always on call. It's a bit like a mixture of being on probation and being a doctor. I would rehearse a couple of mornings a week with the other understudies and a piano and then melt back into the shadows.

Day after day this shadowy existence went on. Tommy seemed fit and well and the chances of me ever going on looked slim. I would dutifully arrive at the stage door thirty-five minutes before show time, collect a glimpse of recognition and report my whereabouts to the stage manager, who wanted to know exactly where I would be at any given time in case I was needed. Fat chance.

I tried to make some use of the time. I would watch the show, go over Tommy's bits in my mind, I even took a course in judo over at the polytechnic opposite. I spent time with two marvellous old timers that I shared a dressing-room with, and listened to them reminisce about the days of Music Hall and Variety. I liked their stories about the Crazy Gang, Lupino Lane and times gone by, one contradicting the other – wonderful characters.

It was a strange existence: not doing much, but always at work, not unlike the window cleaning job. The panto did two shows a day and ran from December till April. Naturally after a month or so of being invisible, my professional standards, like shaving before I went in, started to relax. Besides, you somehow felt tougher at judo if you grappled the instructor with a chin full of bristles.

It was on one of these twilight afternoons – 19 March 1970 to be exact – that the invisible man became the man of the moment. I wandered down Oxford Street, ten minutes late. I was hardly ever late, but no one seemed to notice, so why not? I turned the corner and sauntered into Argyle Street where the Palladium stage door is, and I saw a clack of wardrobe people and stage managers waving and rushing towards me.

'Where have you been?' said Tommy the stage manager. 'You're on. Tommy Steele's sick.' Sick? Not as sick as me, I thought. We trundled *en masse* into Tommy Steele's number one dressing-room, which I noticed was much nicer than my cupboard upstairs.

People were sticking microphones and sound packs on me,

boots and a Dick Whittington costume, and heads were coming round the door instructing me to 'break a leg'. Kenneth O'Connor, my *Carry On* colleague, popped his head round. It was mayhem. Then to top it all, as the dressing-room started to empty, this announcement rang out over the tannoy: 'Due to Tommy Steele being unwell the part of Dick Whittington will be played by David Essex.' The reaction from the audience was a massive 'Who?' and a heart-felt groan – almost as loud as when Chris Waddle missed that penalty for England. Next came the backstage tannoy: 'Beginners, ladies and gentlemen. The part of Dick will be played by David Essex at this performance. Thank you.'

After the rush and the shock, I looked in the mirror and tried to focus. I thought, this is why I've been here, day after day, this is what I'm expected to do. I tried to run the show through in my mind, and then the overture started – coming to my rescue like a source of energy – with snippets of the music in the show. I know it was only 'Little White Bull' and stuff like 'Give a Little Whistle', but it seemed to give me confidence. Now to face the disappointed audience.

I made my entrance to a begrudging round of applause. This was another world from the tin-pot understudy rehearsals I'd been used to. Massive spotlights shone down, blinding my eyes. The sound of the pit orchestra filled the speakers on stage. My mind raced, my knees trembled and as I spoke my first lines I could hear myself through the stage monitors. In short it was surreal.

All seemed to be under control as I finished my first scene. I came off and amid some 'Well Dones' was escorted by a fussy dresser to the dressing-room to change costumes. On my way to the backstage area, I realized that my next entrance came after the dancing bears. At that moment three great big brown bears, poked and prodded by their German trainers, were crashing and growling their way to the stage through a specially built tunnel cage.

Now I'd never met the bears personally or their trainers – this would be another new experience. I changed and waited for my cue to go on. The action, I knew, was that a bear came over and kissed Dick Whittington, then the bears and Germans exited, leaving me to go straight into a song; but what I didn't realize was that the bear was really after a Polo mint secreted in Dick's mouth. As I made my entrance the German lady trainer said, 'Put zis in your mouth.' I obeyed and stood and waited. Sure enough, what seemed to be the biggest bear waddled over to me and through his muzzle searched with his tongue for the mint in my mouth. Unfortunately the mint had gone to the back of my throat and so did the bear's enormous tongue. It was one of the longest French kisses I've ever encountered and most certainly the longest tongue. Not a pleasant experience.

The orchestra started the intro to the next song, ironically 'There's Gotta Be Something Better Than This', a sentiment I was certainly feeling as I was on the verge of gagging as I tried to wipe the bear saliva off my face. Miraculously I somehow made it through the song and was for the first time ever relieved when the dance break came. After that the rest of the performance was a doddle. My interpretations of Tommy's tunes like 'Little White Bull', 'What a Mouth' and 'Flash Bang Wallop' seemed to strike a chord with the matinee audience, and at the curtain call at the end of the show you would have thought a star was born as cries of 'Bravo!' echoed round the auditorium.

I went on another three times for Tommy during the run and each time made sure the Polo mint was firmly gripped between my teeth.

On the recording front I made a few more nearly hit records around this time, including a duet with a black girl called Rozaa. All were written and produced by Arnold, Martin and Morrow, and although the boys did their best, sadly not much happened. I decided that if I was ever going to make another record I'd write the bleeding song myself. I'm glad to say that the boys and I parted company with our goodwill for each other intact. One of the most memorable moments I spent with them was when Man landed on the Moon and David Martin and I went out into his garden, scanning the Moon to see if we could see anyone.

I might have been *over* the moon if I had recorded a song Tony Macauley asked me to do. Having produced a record with me called 'Just for Tonight' for Pye Records, Tony then offered me another song called 'Build Me Up Buttercup' which I turned down as I didn't like the title. He went on to record it with the Foundations and had a massive hit with it all over the world. How was that for judgement? Never judge a book by its cover, or a song by its title.

I also did a residency at The Valbonne Club, a trendy place with an inside swimming pool and a massive fish tank behind the bandstand. Sadly the band's volume killed off the fish, and when the band themselves leaped fully clothed into the pool, messing up the filter system, our residency soon ended.

Derek and I had some thinking to do. Things personally were fine. Maureen and I were going steady, we were even talking of buying a house together, but the recording career was beginning to feel as if we had outstayed our welcome.

After a couple of quiet months Derek called with the offer of another panto, this time in Manchester. No understudying this time. I was to play the part of Dandini in *Cinderella* with Mary Hopkin, Lonnie Donegan and Big-Hearted Arthur Askey. 'Why?' I said.

Apparently the producer had seen my earth-shattering Dick and offered me the job.

Pantomimes, I think, are fascinating, especially backstage where you come across men dressed as women, women dressed as men, dancers dressed in hardly anything, plus the back half of a cow. So I took the job and the compliment and went to Manchester. I rented this bedsit outside the city with its own *en suite* bathroom. The only problem was that it was so cold in the flat that when I took a bath the steam was like one of those pea-souper fogs of my childhood.

My time in Manchester was a little wayward. There were two comics in the show, Dailey and Wayne, who were very Northern and very funny and could drink a very large amount of alcohol, and although I tried not to hang out with them all the time it just seemed to happen.

One evening they decided to take me to a night club – it was Billy Fury's opening night. By the time we'd changed and got there, the place was pretty packed. Some seats were reserved for us at a table with one of their mates, someone I'd never heard of called Freddy Starr. When we sat down the boys pointed to the seats in front, telling me they were occupied by a local team of gangsters nicknamed The Quality Street Gang. I tried to look impressed. The lights dimmed and on rocked Billy Fury, who was sounding good when halfway through the third number, Freddy appeared on stage beside him with a cushion up his back doing a very good impression of poor Billy. This seemed of serious interest to the Quality Street boys and some of them stood up to see, when all of a sudden the boss grabbed a candle from the table and with the words 'I can't bloody see' set fire to one of his colleagues' Afros – WHOOSH went this bloke's hair. He jumped up, smacking himself around the head, and there was no shortage of willing helpers, all whacking his head in a desperate attempt to put it out.

Billy and his mimic soldiered on through 'Halfway to Paradise' but in all honesty only got halfway as all eyes were on the burning bonce and the fight that followed. I felt the same way for Billy as I did for Daddy Dines during the Great Bee Massacre all those years ago.

It was just as well that there was some excitement outside the panto, because the part of Dandini was particularly tedious. Carrying round a glass slipper and singing the odd song with the Prince (Tony Adams, a nice man – later of *Crossroads* fame) was not nearly as exciting as kissing bears, so as we were nearing the end of the run, I thought I'd spice it up.

I went off and bought a pair of Wellingtons, one of which I substituted for the glass slipper in the last scene where we finally track down Cinders. With boot on cushion I marched in and plonked it on Cinders' elegant foot. 'It fits,' I pronounced. The audience roared as the Prince and Cinders sang their love duet, Cinders trying to retain some dignity in her massive Wellington boot.

Mary Hopkins, who played Cinderella, took my prank in good spirit and actually thanked me for livening up Cinders' part, but Big-Hearted Arthur was not too pleased at the laughs it got. Comics can be very possessive of comedy.

# 7

# A House, a Home and a Baby

Cinders finished and I returned home to Essex. In March 1971, Maureen and I started to think about buying a place together. We had both mainly lived at home, although I did rent a bedsit in Earls Court for a time. Both our families thought buying a house was more sensible than paying rent for something we would never own.

Maureen's father, a car dealer, offered to help Maureen with money for a deposit. I had a little money from my Dandini outing, so we found a Victorian terraced house in Seven Kings costing £3,950 and put down a deposit. It had three bedrooms and a small back garden and we loved it. To help with the mortgage payments we rented a room to Kath and her boyfriend Michael, and tried to make ends meet. I was signing on and Maureen was delivering flowers and bringing in money.

Derek and I were starting to think that maybe we were never going to get the luck we felt we deserved. A pile of near-miss singles had come out over a five-year period; bits and pieces in film and theatre had not set the world alight, and a serious reality check came when Maureen announced she was pregnant.

It was time, I thought, to get a real job. With the responsibility of a child on the way, I felt I should provide for the little person. I started to scan the papers for a job – anything that had some freedom to it, like lorry driving or something.

The relationship between me and Derek had become cooler lately. I suppose I resented our lack of success, and although of course I couldn't blame him for it, there was a coldness in our conversations. I was starting to feel that I'd sold my soul for shows and other people's songs that I didn't totally believe in. After all, I hadn't wanted to leave the drums anyway.

With a baby on the way, Maureen and I decided to get married. We chose a simple local Registry Office wedding. We loved each other and our main concern was the coming baby and not to waste money that we didn't have. My old mate Frank was the best man and our one extravagance was provided by Maureen's dad – a white Rolls-Royce to ferry us to the Registry Office and back.

So there I was – married, unemployed and very broke. I spent most of my time doing up the house. My experience of painting factories came in useful. I even replaced the windows. I was in fact hanging out of a window when Derek rang. Taking the phone I reluctantly agreed to attend an audition. In my mind I truly thought, 'This is the very last time.' I even questioned the title of the show, 'Godspell'.

'Gospel, you mean?' I said curtly to dear Derek.

I was called to the Globe Theatre for eleven a.m. the following Thursday. So was the rest of the world; there were hundreds of hopefuls there. It was the early afternoon when I was finally called on stage. You can imagine my enthusiasm was wearing thin as a soft-spoken, bearded American hippy in overalls bade me welcome. 'What will you sing?' the piano player asked. 'Going Out of My Head' seemed a reasonable choice.

And away I went. 'Could we hear another kind of music-hall type song?' OK – I hit them with that Tommy Steele favourite 'What a Mouth'. This seemed to go down a treat, they took my phone number and said they would call me. Yeah, I bet you will, I thought, as I walked to the Underground.

The weekend passed and so did Monday. That's that, I thought, and made an appointment for a job interview for van driving. I'd done some minicab driving for an eccentric owner, who used to put on his wig whenever someone came in for a cab. That was until the office got petrol-bombed by a competitor.

I used to have to do the twilight shifts, like ten p.m. to four a.m. It's amazing the people you meet at that time. First, the pubs turn out, which probably meant someone throwing up down the back of your neck or ten or twelve drunks all trying to get into your cab at the same time. Then it would mellow out to weirdo time. I had a man that I would pick up who had trouble sleeping and just wanted to drive round the streets for an hour in his pyjamas. A woman who, when I took south of the river and asked for the fare, pulled down her knickers and said, 'Take it out of that.'

One very weird occasion I remember was the night when I picked up a man in Hornchurch to be taken to a place called Wharley Hospital. As we drove through the dark lanes of Essex my passenger suddenly jumped out of the back seat and started climbing into the front seat, using my head as a lever. I pushed him off and back into the rear seat and was just getting a little concerned when up ahead I saw the sign for the hospital. Then it clicked. Michael, my troubled friend, had been on weekend leave from a psychiatric hospital.

As we entered the gates the place was in near darkness, a big scary neogothic building silhouetted in the moonlight. I locked Michael in the car and went to look for life.

I found a hallway with a light on and rang the bell. Through the window I could see some of the inmates walking about, or just rocking from side to side. Fittingly it was a man in a white coat who opened the door. I explained that I had Michael in the car. 'He's very late,' barked the gaoler and we made our way to the car. Michael by this time had got into the front seat and was attempting to climb through a crack in the window I had left open for his convenience. He cringed when he saw the white-coated one but allowed himself to be led back into the hospital with me following behind. Once inside, I asked poor Michael for the fare.

'Where is it, Michael? Where's your money?' said the man.

Michael pathetically opened a tobacco tin and held out six-pence. I looked at his frightened eyes and said, 'It's all right. Forget it.' The man in the white coat was not ready to forget it and shouted at a trembling Michael. It was awful. I left, leaving poor Michael to his nightmare.

I had just started to decorate what would be the baby's room when the phone rang. Maureen picked it up and gave me a shout. As I put the paintbrush down I wondered if it was about a recall for that *Godspell* thing – but it was just to confirm my interview at the van driving depot. Right, I thought, a cup of tea and I'll tackle the ceiling. The phone rang again, and this time it *was* the *Godspell* thing. A recall was arranged which means in audition terms that you have made it to a short list. How long the short list is, is anybody's guess, but it was positive news.

I made my way to the Prince of Wales Theatre, and this time the numbers had been dramatically cut. There were about twenty or so boys and girls on this short list, and after a communal warm-up, we were put through some 'trust-enhancing' exercises with the group, things like falling off a table and trusting the others to catch you, or leading a partner through the streets outside. One would keep their eyes shut and let the open-eyed one lead them through the deadly traffic.

It was a long session, in which we sang, danced, mimed, became trees and animals – the lot. Some of this I was uncomfortable with, especially doing monkeys, but I kept going. We all received sincere thanks from the director John Michael Tebelak and the composer Stephen Schwartz, said farewell and hoped for the best.

By the time I got back to Seven Kings, Derek had already called. The *Godspell* producers had been in touch and were thinking of casting me in the role of John the Baptist, who becomes Judas in the second act. Apparently they were talking to the actor Murray Head for the part of Jesus.

As the next few days and many phone calls unfolded, Derek sensed there was a split in the producers' camp regarding who to cast as Jesus. As I understood it later, Stephen Schwartz wanted me to be the chosen one, maintaining that throughout the ensemble work on stage the person who caught his eye time after time was me. John Michael was stuck on Murray. Then by a twist of fate, Murray was offered a film and decided to do it, which made me the unanimous choice for Jesus.

I'll never forget my first meeting after being cast, when John Michael and Stephen were trying to explain the attitude of the production. 'We play Jesus as a red-nosed clown,' John Michael enthused. These people could be barmy, I thought.

The first day of rehearsal arrived and I met the other nine clowns that would enter into this extraordinary theatrical adventure.

The girls were Julie Covington, Marti Webb, Verity-Ann Meldrum, Gay Soper, and Jacquie-Ann Carr. The boys were Neil Fitzwilliam, Deryk Parkin, Tom Saffery and Jeremy Irons, who was to play the John the Baptist and Judas part. They had also cast two understudies, Liz Whiting and Christopher Scoular.

I'm not sure that the Americans realized quite what a formidable cast they had assembled.

When the news broke that the first portrayal of Jesus ever to grace the West End stage would be played as a red-nosed clown, and by a docker's son to boot, there was uproar. Up until that time there had been a ban on playing Jesus in the West End and the fact that just after the censorship was lifted Christ was to be played for the first time in this seemingly irreverent way upset a lot of people. I received letters from people informing me I would burn in hell, and there was a controversial response from the media too.

My feeling is that the telling of the gospel according to Saint Matthew in *Godspell* did much to strip away the ritualistic glitter and trimmings that abound in organized religion and made Jesus the prophet, man and teacher more accessible. Through irony, pathos and almost music-hall style routines, we seemed to touch people in a very real way.

As the storm raged around us, the cast and I kept our heads down and continued rehearsing.

Rehearsals with John Michael were quite unusual. A young man in his mid twenties, he was more of a gentle organizer than a strong director. We would throw in ideas, try them, keep them if they worked and discard them if they didn't. As rehearsals went on, it felt as if the show was slowly starting to belong to us; we believed in it, and it was like directing our own show.

Usually, if you're lucky you get six weeks to stage a musical. Our rehearsals were going on and on without a definite opening date. As we found out later, the show was supposed to open at the Prince of Wales theatre, but midway through the rehearsals a spy from the company that owned the theatre had come down, seen these ten over-active hippies and withdrawn the theatre. This of course had thrown the producers into a panic. As they beavered away to find a theatre to open in, we just kept rehearsing. I think we were in our eighth week when Joe Beruh, one of the producers, called us together. Joe, a New York Jew and someone I liked and trusted, explained the position.

Basically it was depressing news: we had a show but nowhere to stage it. There was a chance, he went on, of opening for a short season at a venue in Chalk Farm, North London called the Roundhouse, and he and the other two producers, Edgar

Lansbury (brother of Angela) and Stuart Duncan (who had something to do with Worcester sauce) were attempting to tie up the
pieces.

The Roundhouse is a fine old railway building, large and circular, made of iron, where train engines were turned around in days
gone by. By this time, in the early 1970s, it had become a kind of
arty experimental place. It was a long way from the glamour and
glitz of the West End and the Prince of Wales.

To be honest most of the cast were not that disappointed with
the change of venue – we just wanted to open the thing. There
were a few exceptions. I remember Jacquie-Ann Carr felt the
Roundhouse was slumming it, but she was probably the most
showbiz of us all; Marti, who had worked many times in the West
End, was a little worried about life in Chalk Farm; but for the rest
of us I think it took some of the pressure off a West End opening.
The producers secured the Roundhouse and, shortly after, we
moved in.

I loved the Roundhouse. It was a basic and earthy place where
creative people would congregate. The auditorium was in the
round, of course, which meant some tinkering with the staging,
but the place seemed to me to suit the wire fence set and the four-
piece rock band, housed in towers above the stage.

An opening night was set for 17 November 1971, so after a
long rehearsal period we were on our way. It's always a thrill
when the musicians arrive for the first time. The line-up was
drums, bass guitar, lead guitar and keyboards. They breathed life
into Stephen Schwartz's very strong score and lifted the cast, who
were on the verge of being over-rehearsed.

I will never forget that opening night. Outside there were
protesters with placards; inside the reaction from the audience was
overwhelming. I actually remember glancing behind me to see
why they were laughing, then realized they were reacting to the
stuff we had put together. The climax, though, was the crucifixion

scene. As I was carried headlong through the auditorium I could hear men and women sobbing, some uncontrollably.

After the triumphant first night there were queues of people lining the Roundhouse trying to buy tickets, and the producers were offered three West End theatres to transfer to in the first week. It was like having your own show become successful.

I don't think anyone, except those connected to it, expected the show to be such a massive hit. Even the wrath of the religious zealots was beginning to abate. Some of the reviews I received personally were, as Derek said, better than he had ever seen. That lengendary critic the late Harold Hobson described my portrayal of Christ as worthy of Michelangelo. I was very hot and so was the show.

Maureen was now eight months' pregnant and the Archbishop of Canterbury upon hearing my wife was pregnant, offered personally to baptise the unborn child. We didn't take him up on it. It was now mid-December and I was starting to wonder, as we were coming up to Christmas, if Maureen and I should change our names to Mary and Joseph.

On 18 December, Maureen went into the early stages of labour so we packed her bag and I took her to the hospital in an old beaten-up Mercedes I had bought for £150. I stayed for an hour or so till she was settled, and asked her if she wanted me to stay. She insisted I went off to do the show, as there was no way of knowing when the baby would arrive. I left for the Roundhouse, my thoughts with them both.

There were two shows that particular day, and in a world without mobile phones I asked our company manager and good friend Tony Howell to keep in touch with the hospital and give me any news. I found it very difficult that day to focus on the show, which had a dreamlike quality to it. In the interval we used to invite the audience on to the stage for some wine, but being preoccupied I was finding it difficult to talk to people. Many would ask the usual questions. Did I believe in Jesus? Did I think he was the Son of God? I always tried to be as sensitive as possible to all the questions asked, as after all, we were dealing with people's innermost beliefs, and who really knows the truth? With overwhelming thoughts of Maureen and the nipper, I left the stage to see if there was any news. Tony had spoken to the hospital – Maureen was OK, but no sign of the baby yet, he said.

On we went with the second act and into the break between shows. It was a strange feeling, worried and excited all at the same time. Midway through the first act of the second show I felt a change in the atmosphere on stage, and the eyes of the cast all seemed to be on me. Then a note was passed to me under the wire fence which simply said, 'You can father a son but you have to be a father to a daughter.'

I was a Father, I had a Daughter. I was so very happy...I never had a chance to come in with my next line as I was surrounded by the cast, all of whom seemed oblivious to the bemused audience. The girls were crying and the boys looked as happy as me. If you were in the audience on 18 December 1971 I hope you forgive us.

Rushing back to the hospital after the show I went through a red light just as it changed and was pulled over by a policeman. I explained that I was sorry and had not seen the light, and I was just about to give him the reason why I was in a rush, when he replied, 'Well, Jesus wouldn't lie, would he? Off you go.' My fame was spreading.

I finally got to the ward, and there she was – the most wonderful thing I had ever seen. Little Verity, Verity Leigh.

Not the second coming after all, not a boy born on 25 December, but a beautiful, magical, brilliant baby girl.

Maureen had a tough time with a long hard labour so she spent a few more days in hospital. I would visit and finish off preparations for the homecoming.

A very special Christmas was upon us, with mother and baby home safely, doting grandparents and family – it was great.

After the Christmas break, it was time to go back to the show. When we all got back I proudly showed off photographs of Verity, probably to everyone in the theatre. I'm surprised I didn't show them to the audience at the interval.

Tony Howell broke the news that the producers and their English co-producers, H.M. Tennent, had decided that the show would move on 25 January to the Wyndham's Theatre. So I would after all be the first actor to portray Jesus on the West End stage.

I was sad to leave the Roundhouse, as it had been a special three months. I'd gotten a taste for vegetarian food and for the first time tasted a brownie not to mention really exotic food like your taramasalata. Each night I would get home about 12.30 a.m. and usually be the one to feed and change the baby at about three or four in the morning. It was sometimes hard to get up, but I treasured those times. It seemed as if Verity and I were the only two people in the world. I would watch her little face, hold her tiny fingers and pretend that wind was actually a smile for her daddy.

Everything was fine and dandy, both at home and in my career. The move to Wyndham's went very well, and I received another batch of glowing reviews. *Godspell* was the hottest ticket in town. *The Sunday Times* wrote: 'This inward happiness, this fragility, a joyous wine in a frail vessel is the mark of David Essex's Jesus in *Godspell*. This Jesus is a man who has found a splendid treasure and is eager to share it with everyone he meets. He is an agile but cheerful debater, with a ready answer to all objections, and a touching confidence.

'There have been many Christs in the world of art; the tormented Christ of El Greco, the benign shepherd of Murillo, the bland Christ of Rubens, the soaring Christ in majesty of Epstein;

and Mr Essex's gentle and innocent figure, as capable of infinite and simple affection as it is incapable of seeing evil anywhere, is worthy to rank with them. There is no point in not speaking one's mind. I do not forget the tremendous goings-on at the New Theatre, but it is my firm opinion that Mr Essex's is the best performance in London, the least histrionic, the happiest, and the most moving. That it should be so at a time when we all marvel at Olivier's prodigious James Tyrone, one of our greatest actor's finest creations, is a measure of Mr Essex's achievement.'

I think it means the boy done good!

I and the rest of the cast were now becoming the toast of the town. After being viewed initially with suspicion by the Church, we were invited to perform a segment of the show in St Paul's Cathedral. We were invited to after-show parties with the rich and powerful, but through it all, we stuck together. I have never been in a show where a cast was so united. I suppose the fact that it was very much an ensemble show had a lot to do with it.

I had signed a contract to appear in *Godspell* for eighteen months, and the way things were going, it was going to run that long and far beyond. There was no doubt that Derek and I were breaking through, ironically with a piece of theatre rather than with music as I had imagined. Then a chance encounter helped to set me off on the pop music trail again.

Liz Whiting, one of the understudies, had an American boyfriend named Jeff Wayne. Jeff had come over with his father, Jerry, to work on a musical called *A Tale of Two Cities*, and stayed. He had settled in a mews house near Baker Street, writing and producing music for television advertisements. I was also impressed by the fact that Jeff was one of the writers of 'Martian Hop', which may have sown the seeds for *War of the Worlds* and his brush with martians later.

One day Jeff, who was a fan of the show, asked if I would like to sing on an advert. I agreed, thinking OK, it's only a jingle, but it's back to where I came from – music. I went in and sang a jingle for Pledge furniture polish – making more money from a ten-minute recording session than I did in three months of playing Jesus, which I thought, even then, was kind of obscene.

Jeff and I got on well and decided to form a band for fun. Jeff played keyboards, and a couple of session musicians joined the line-up. Marti Webb and Julie Covington were our backing singers and we would do the odd Sunday night gig.

I remember one show we did at the Revolution Club to a sparse audience. I was half-way through Paul McCartney's 'Long and Winding Road' when I noticed Paul sitting right in front of me. Being the gracious man he is, he applauded enthusiastically.

I did a couple of other jingles for Jeff and enjoyed doing them, but really I was keen to get back to music, on my own terms this time. *Godspell* and the springboard it had given me meant there was predictable interest in me from the recording world again. Both the *Godspell* cast album and a single from the show, 'Day by Day', were in the top ten, but my personal ambition for the future was to record my own songs and develop my own sound.

Four or five months after *Godspell* opened, another musical featuring Jesus opened down the road from us – *Jesus Christ Superstar*. This led to a media frenzy, as comparisons between the two shows and the two portrayals of Christ – which was better and so on and so on – became the flavour of the month.

*Godspell* and I seemed to come out unscathed in these comparisons, probably because we were a simple show where only the clowns set the mood. Our set was a wire fence, three planks, two saw horses and a wooden crate to stand on in the crucifixion scene, whereas *Jesus Christ Superstar* was a big spectacle with massive sets and costumes.

The media did their bit to provoke rivalry between the shows, but in reality there was none. We respected and knew most of the actors in *Superstar*, and I think they respected us. I remember a

BBC television debate between Tim Rice and myself called *Box Office Christ* where the plan, it seemed, was to fire up a bit of friction and controversy between us. In reality it started a wonderful friendship between Sir Tim and me that has lasted thirty years and that I hope will go on for thirty more. Slowly both shows were accepted for their own merits. Tim wearing a *Godspell* T-shirt that Jeremy and I sent him and me wearing a *Superstar* one must have helped.

Since my success with *Godspell*, the papers and teen magazines were featuring me in a regular way, and the stage door was crowded with people waiting for autographs or photographs and, occasionally, deep theological discussions.

Covent Garden in those days was still a working vegetable and flower market. It was good to walk through it after the show as it began to spring into life. The earthiness and good humour of the porters reminded me of the dockers back home. Most nights Jeremy Irons and I used to go to an Italian restaurant called Luigi's for a meal after the show. It was like going round to your mum's. These were happy and exciting times.

Considering our age and how successful the show was, the cast were very professional and although we had been doing it for about six months rarely did we get up to mischief on stage, although one exception does spring to mind. One night, after Jeremy came on stage to baptize me at the beginning of the show, I looked into his eyes – which were closed – and he had written 'Fuck off' on his eyelids. It took me half of my first song, 'God Save the People', to stop giggling.

# 8

# That'll Be the Day

Derek was slowly being snowed under with requests for his hot new actor. Interviews, TV appearances, photo sessions – there was hardly enough time in the day to do them all. The fact that I was doing eight performances a week in a very energetic show, not to mention my sleepless nights with baby Verity, meant we were very selective.

Then came an offer which, as they say, we could not refuse. David Puttnam, a film producer, approached me to do a screen test for a film he wanted to make. I was told it was going to be about a working-class boy, growing up in the Fifties, who decides at the end of the film that he wants to be a Rock Star. I went one afternoon to Hampstead, met up with David, the director Claude Whatham, a film crew and an actress. We then found a suitable location by a tree on the Heath and shot a short scene, after which I was driven back to the theatre for the evening show.

By now I had read the script and liked it. I was also impressed by the proposed line-up for the film: Ringo Starr, Keith Moon and Billy Fury (hopefully without Freddie Starr this time) were already cast. Within forty-eight hours of the screen test a firm offer from Goodtimes Enterprises – the company run by David Puttnam and his partner Sandy Lieberson – reached Derek's busy telephone.

We were pleased, but we had a problem. I was contracted to play Jesus for eighteen months and had only played about five. We needed permission to leave *Godspell* to star in the film.

Derek hastily arranged a meeting with the head of H.M. Tennent, the formidable Hugh Beaumont, known as Binky – I wonder if he'd met Bunny? Binky was an impressive upper-class sounding impresario in the Noël Coward mode (Mr Coward by the way came to see *Godspell* and hated it). Derek and I entered his office and explained the position.

Binky ruminated, then gave us a glimmer of hope, hatching a formula which he thought might work. First he said he had to get the agreement of the American co-producers, but his idea was that he would give me three months' leave to make the film in return for an extra six months on my *Godspell* contract, which meant basically two years of playing Jesus.

Derek and I left to consider. Derek felt it was a bit like blackmail, but I was intent on making the film. We agreed to wait until the Americans had agreed with Binky's proposal before we made a final decision.

In the meantime there were many persuasive calls from the film company, and when the Americans finally agreed to Binky's proposal, we did too. *That'll Be the Day* started filming on location on the Isle of Wight on 23 October 1972.

The script was by a former *Liverpool Echo* journalist called Ray Connolly. It was about people in their teens growing up in the late Fifties during the first flush of youth culture, to a background of the first rock'n'roll music and its idols, a film about the environment and influences that sowed the seeds in young boys' minds that later created the Beatles, The Who, the Rolling Stones and many of those great Sixties writers and groups.

Set at a time when all the credible influences were coming from America, this film was about characters that lived through them and had the confidence to create their own identity that would be part of the force that took back youth culture and placed it firmly in 1960s Britain, with its centre firmly in London. I thought the film was worthwhile then, and when I've watched it since, I have always been struck by its honesty.

Making the film was nearly too much fun. Maureen, Verity and I found a nice little house in Shanklin on the Isle of Wight for the seven-week shoot, and although it wasn't a holiday, it was pretty close.

When filming you are called at some unearthly times – 5.30 in the morning was pretty usual. It took a week or so to adjust my body clock, as I was used to doing evening shows. Also the waiting around while filming is endless. To retain concentration as you sit in your caravan hour upon hour is really the key to being a film actor. Actors in films do not have the control they have in the theatre. Film, I think, remains a directors' medium.

The great thing about *That'll Be the Day* was that the cast were cool to be with. Ringo was easy-going and funny, Keith Moon eccentric and publicly manic. I remember Keith's arrival by helicopter. The landing pad, the hotel roof, was marked out with table-cloths to direct the pilot, but the formidable force of the chopper's downdraft blew the table-cloths away, sending Italian waiters in a frenzy on to the beach below in an attempt to retrieve them before dinner time. Keith emerged from the helicopter announcing, 'The only way to travel, dear boy. I was on my front lawn in Chertsey twenty minutes ago and now I'm here. Where's the bar?'

I liked Keith very much, and in his quiet moments found him to be intelligent and caring. In public, he was like a gun-slinger with a reputation for swinging on chandeliers, so rather than let people down – he did.

The hotel where the cast and some of the crew were staying was a lively place. Harry Nilsson always seemed to be there, I'm not sure why. We had jam sessions most nights, which were interesting with three drummers in the cast. Sometimes we left directly from a fairly wild all-nighter straight on to the early morning film set. As I was in nearly every scene, I tried to keep a lid on my own behaviour and did my best to manage my madness. I would attempt to get back to the house in Shanklin, and a few hours' sleep, but sometimes I failed.

Filming on the Isle of Wight was really good, even though it was the early Seventies and like many English seaside places, there was still an air of the Fifties about the place. All the extras in the film were local people, which probably explains why, when the film was released there, it ran for months. Everybody lined up to see themselves, friends and relations in the movies.

After seven weeks on the Isle of Wight, filming continued at Pinewood Studios. It was there that I first had the idea for the song 'Rock On'. I was waiting as usual in my dressing-room, when I began thinking about the film's subject-matter and what a big influence Fifties Americana had on the teenagers in Britain. I started to write down some images – James Dean, 'Blue Suede Shoes', 'Summertime Blues'. One idea led to another, and even as I wrote the lyrics I could hear a melody in my head. 'Rock On' was one of the quickest songs I've ever written and one of the most successful.

Upon finishing the film I'd started to write songs on a more regular basis. I was back with my friends in *Godspell* and felt fresh after the break. I was still getting together with Jeff Wayne and our Sunday band, and it was after one of our get-togethers that I told Jeff I was now writing with a view to recording an album. Jeff said he would like to hear the songs, so I sang a song I had just finished called 'On and On'. Jeff really liked it, then, as if by mutual agreement, I said, 'You work in the studio, why don't you produce it and I'll write it?' And that's how our partnership was born. Not knowing what publishing really was, I gave the publishing rights of my songs to Jeff for free. Derek was horrified.

We decided to go in to Advision Studios and record two songs, 'Rock On' and 'On and On'. Jeff, as I would learn, always had a potent combination of musicality and experimentation in his arrangements. I sang 'On and On' live with the rhythm section, all terrific players who would contribute so much to the David Essex sound. This was the line-up: drums – Barry DeSousa; bass – Herbie Flowers; percussion – Ray Cooper; guitar – Chris Spedding.

The song went down nicely and the plan was to record the other orchestral instruments at a later session. Our attention now turned to 'Rock On'. Jeff had sketched out not much more than a framework, which the boys and I ran through. A shape was beginning to come, when Herbie the bass player said, 'What about this?' and played what would become one of the most lengendary bass lines in modern music and the spark of 'Rock On'.

We laid down a very sparse backing track with my lead vocal. I suggested to the engineer Gary Martin that he put a Fifties-style tape echo on my voice. This, together with the bass line, started to create the atmosphere of the record. Jeff took the recordings and went away to do the arrangements for the orchestral session. A week later it was exciting to hear the orchestra playing 'On and On' for the first time, a song that I had written, and Jeff had done a good job.

Jeff thanked most of the musicians and for 'Rock On' just asked the string section to stay. Then the fun started. We wanted to loosen up these classically trained musicians, so a few bottles of wine were brought in. We knew we wanted something different to suit 'Rock On', and we wanted to experiment. Jeff got them to de-tune, or play slightly out of tune, which wasn't too difficult as the wine was flowing fast. The final effect was this Indian mantra sound which features in the instrumental section of the record.

We felt we still needed something to compliment the strings, an unusual sound. Jeff knew a brass player called Derek Wadsworth who dabbled on the didgeridoo, so he called him, and Derek turned up with a didgeridoo tied on top of his station wagon and gave it a go. Jeff and I listened intently, turned to each other and collapsed on the floor laughing – this thing was as tuneful as a giant blow-off!

Luckily Derek had a rather nifty electric trombone with him that worked a treat, so we used that instead. Then backing singers were added and we prepared to mix the tracks. Gary Martin the engineer created a wonderful quality of sound, using repeat echoes and landmark stereo effects. Between us all, we had created something special.

When the track was finished, Jeff had the idea of presenting it to David Puttnam for use in *That'll Be the Day*. In fact David turned it down, saying it was too weird, but later he included 'Rock On' in the *That'll Be the Day* album of music featured in the film.

Things were very busy. Interviews, photo sessions, fans at the Wyndham's stage door, and the film hadn't even come out yet. I was writing when I could, spending as much time as possible with Verity and Maureen – Verity was now walking after taking her first steps on the Isle of Wight – and I was still playing Jesus eight times a week.

There seemed to be massive interest in the film even before it opened, and when it did, on 12 April 1973, it soon became the hottest film in Britain, breaking box-office records and generally being acclaimed. Ringo was quite rightly recognized as a decent actor, and I was starting to be propelled into another strato-sphere. The soundtrack album, including 'Rock On', was number one in the album charts for weeks. Derek had his work cut out to manage Managing.

I remember Jeremy Irons reflecting on my growing fame and his relative obscurity as we sat having dinner as usual at Luigi's, and me reassuring him that it was only a matter of time before something would happen for him. It was evident then what a fine actor he was.

But I never felt any jealousy from the cast. They were supportive and protective. The 'wine with the audience' intervals though were starting to become a little crazy and sadly sometimes when I was swamped I had to take refuge and leave the stage. The show itself was now bringing in a much more varied audience, including people who wouldn't normally go to the theatre as well as the sort of theatre-goers that I used to sit alongside with Derek in the early days. In short, it was lively.

With our upturn in fortunes, the girls and I had sold the house in Seven Kings and had moved up to a new town house with a country aspect in Chigwell Row. I'd bought a second-hand convertible Mercedes for £1,750, which I still own today, and Maureen a Renault Four to ferry Verity and herself around.

With all that was going on, various record companies were chasing me. I'd signed to Jeff's production company, so the approaches now came through him. Columbia Records, or CBS as they were known in England, seemed to be the front runners, headed by an American ex-lawyer named Dick Asher. I remember many transatlantic phone negotiations. After weighing up our many options, Derek, Jeff and I felt there was a genuine commitment from Dick Asher and Columbia Records and signed a five-album deal with CBS.

Immediately I was faced with my first battle. There was a feeling around the record company that for my first single release 'Rock On' might be too avant-garde. I stood my ground, having learned from the past. I was determined to make the kind of musical statement I wanted to make. 'On and On' was a nice record, but I wanted 'Rock On' as the A side. Jeff stood by me and we won the war. CBS never interfered on the creative side again.

To announce their signing and the release of 'Rock On', CBS held a reception on 16 August 1973 at Quaglino's. *That'll Be the Day* was now on general release, and of course my song 'Rock On' was part of a long-standing number one album, so the reception in the ballroom at Quaglino's was packed. It seemed that all of the music business was there. I left them to it as I had *Godspell* to do, but it was evident that David Essex was the Man of the Moment – even the picture on the record sleeve was taken by photographic legend David Bailey.

With 'Rock On' released, momentum began to build. It seemed that, not unlike the character I was playing, I could walk on water.

Record reviews for the single were good – 'More than just a pretty face,' said one, 'more than a slender waist, this man has the guts to put out a positively thirst-quenching hit 45 – a rumble of bass, a voice laced in reverb and a glance back to blue jeans, baby queens, and James Dean. A feat of subtleties – it will mess with your head.'

At the record shop signings I did to promote the single, 'Essex Mania' was taking hold. I remember we stopped the traffic in Bond Street and lay besieged in Lewisham High Street.

The Lewisham Record Shop Siege was quite something. There must have been two thousand or more teenagers inside and outside the shop. For safety, the shop manager had locked me in the store room, and even when the police arrived it was impossible to get out of the place. Steve Collier, our promotion man, or plugger as they are called, hit on an idea to get me out.

Steve amassed some dustbin lids and, using them as shields, we made a break for the car. The screaming and the force of emotion from the crowd was awesome, but apart from a few dents in our dustbin lids, we managed to escape to the car, unscathed. I got to Wyndham's with only ten minutes to spare.

It was now the middle of August and my date for finally leaving

*Godspell*, 15 September 1973, was on the horizon. People were paying big amounts for tickets on the black market to see me before I left, and obviously the producers were looking for a replacement. In *That'll Be the Day* I had worked with another young actor called Robert Lindsay, who played the college boy, while I played the rebel. I suggested Robert for the part of Jesus, and I'm glad to say that when I left, Robert took over.

During my final week of the show, *That'll Be the Day* was still going strong and playing extended runs not only in the Isle of Wight but in cinemas all over Britain; to get a ticket for *Godspell* was almost impossible; and 'Rock On' had reached number one in the *New Musical Express* singles chart. It was extraordinary to be so successful in three mediums. At the risk of blowing my own trumpet, I don't know of any artiste who has done that. To succeed on all three fronts was a testimony to Derek's belief and foresight.

Although I was weary of playing Jesus in *Godspell* – after all I did it for nearly two years – I didn't realize how emotional the parting with the show and my dear friends would be. In the musical there's a scene that represents the Last Supper where each clown in his or her individual way, bids farewell to Jesus. My last performance was emotionally charged enough, but when the goodbyes came it was heartbreaking.

We had conquered the theatre world together as one. From those first days, when we led our partners, with their eyes closed, through the traffic of London, and our trust in each other began to develop, we had gone on to become, as one, an unstoppable force.

For my first album, *Rock On*, I wrote a song in tribute to the experience of *Godspell* and my final performance, which I called 'September 15th'.

I never have experienced a closeness and a showbiz journey like *Godspell*, and I suspect I never will again.

# 9

# My Life Hanging on a Bedroom Wall

My feet now were hardly touching the ground. For a month or two I'd been writing and recording my first album, then leaving the studio in the evening to do the show. Now that I'd finished *Godspell* it seemed that every day was filled with press interviews and photo sessions, or dotted with TV appearances.

My first *Top of the Pops* I remember well. In those days and for a long time due to some rule from the Musicians' Union, you had to re-record the track you were doing or play it live using the resident musicians. Time was short, and results tended to be mediocre when you did the whole thing live. Jeff and I always tried to opt for the re-recorded backing track and for me to sing live, mainly because a lot of our recordings had a sound about them that was not always easy to reproduce with harassed musicians and sound men who had one eye on the clock.

*Top of the Pops* in those days was probably the most important pop show in the world, and the producer was elevated to a ridiculous level. If he decided to book you for the show it usually meant chart success, so you can imagine how record companies and pluggers swarmed like bees round a honey pot, to curry favour with the great man. Getting booked tended to be easier if you had a record with legs, as we had with 'Rock On' and many other hits later. An appearance on the show guaranteed that nearly every family in

Britain would see and hear and even discuss your performance and the charts at work or school the next morning. A long way from today, when even most teenagers don't know who is in the charts.

Anyway, with 'Rock On' selling ship loads, Robin Nash the producer succumbed and booked me for the show, I arrived at Television Centre and rehearsed to the re-recorded backing track, wearing what I thought would be OK – a black sleeveless T-shirt and black jeans. We were half-way through when Robin stopped the rehearsal and came down from the gallery.

'What are you wearing, David?' he said with a voice of authority.

'I'd thought I'd wear this,' I replied.

'You will disappear into the background, dear,' Mr Nash informed me. No discussion with regard to changing the background. No, a change of clothes was called for.

'Have you nothing white?' Robin enquired. Back home I had an off-white suit. I called Maureen, who dug it out for me, and a car was dispatched to Essex to get it. Robin was much happier with the off-white number. Strangely, the White Suit became a David Essex trade mark, but completely by accident.

Derek, my manager, had now earned the complete respect of all would-be multi-media managers for his guidance on the film, theatre and record front. But he was finding that just keeping up with the demand was nearly impossible. It was time to expand.

Derek had been running operations alone from his home in Harlow but now really needed help. We needed a special person, someone loyal whom we could trust. I remembered a gracious lady who was working for the *Godspell* producer Binky Beaumont. She was unflappable and thorough but, most importantly, like a ray of sunshine. Her name was Madge.

Derek and I decided to approach her and ask her to become my Personal Assistant. As it happened Binky sadly died, and his company was taken over by someone Madge did not particularly get on with. I'm pleased to say she accepted the challenge and joined us, and is still with me today.

Next we looked for a London office and found a small mews building in St John's Wood, just around the corner from the famous Abbey Road Studios. With Madge now on board and an office to work from, we were able to tread water in what were fast becoming hectic times. The film and single were now being released world-wide, with pretty much the same success as in the UK. I was bouncing around all over Europe doing press interviews, TV appearances, photo shoots and attending the odd *That'll Be the Day* film premiere. I especially liked the ones where the local film distributors had over-dubbed the film in their own language. Ringo and me speaking fluent German or Japanese is truly something to behold.

Back home, sadly, I was getting to see Verity and Maureen less and less and I must say I found this difficult, but like a line from a film I made – 'It's like a roller coaster and you can't get off.' After six years of struggling in the wilderness, I was now the chosen one. Teen and music papers carried posters and interviews and seemed to have a insatiable appetite for everything I said and did.

Most of the photographs that started to appear on bedroom walls were taken by an old friend of mine, Colin Davey. Colin was actually an apprentice with me, but unlike me he finished his apprenticeship, then left electrical engineering to become a photographer. We would try to get together as often as possible to satisfy the demand from the media, not in a posh studio like David Bailey's but wherever we could. We regularly used the home studio of a friend of Colin's in Leytonstone, until the local kids found out I was there and put us under siege. These were easy-going photo sessions between two friends that usually finished up with us both in stitches as Colin attempted to direct me from behind his camera. Just the mention of 'Look serious' or 'Look sexy' would send us into fits of laughter.

With the album finished and a new single scheduled for UK release, Maureen, Verity and I had moved further into the Essex countryside. We bought a nice house in Havering-Atte-Bower, reputed to have parts of Henry the Eighth's hunting lodge in it. It gave us the privacy we were looking for, but was still within striking distance of our parents. Just after moving into the house, a promotional trip was scheduled to America. I was really excited about going to the states for the first time and experiencing Americana first hand. 'Rock On' and *That'll Be the Day* had just been released. The film was struggling a little due to lack of general release, but the record was starting to break ground. Derek and I travelled to eleven major cities in fourteen days and all I really saw were radio stations, journalists and receptions. It was my first time in America, and although I'd travelled the length and breadth of it, it was disappointing to see so little of it.

I remember the US perception of me was different from the 'teen idol' thing that was starting in Europe. The Americans had seen the film, heard the record and immediately came to the conclusion that I was a credible force, something that the British media were mixed about. It's never been easy for the media in this country as far as I was concerned, because although their wish was to put me in the 'teen idol' pigeon-hole, the work I did, plus the fact that I wrote my own songs, had them confused. I remember being the darling of music's most cutting edge paper at that time, the *New Musical Express*, appearing on its front page with glowing write-ups – only to be discarded a year or so later as the success snowballed and more and more pin-ups appeared in the teen magazines. In fact a review for one of my later albums said, and I quote: 'On this album Essex sounds like a constipated stoat.' Your guess is as good as mine.

With regard to how seriously I was taken in the US, I remember doing an interview for the most famous of all music papers,

*Rolling Stone,* in which a John Lennon look-alike journalist talked about how profound my lyrics were for 'Rock On'. He asked if the bridge section which contains the lines 'And where do we go from here? Which is the way that's clear?' really was about a post-Vietnam generation searching for direction. He was visibly shaken when I replied, 'No, it just rhymed.'

Upon my return in November 1973 from the whistle-stop tour of America, 'Lamplight', the second single, and the *Rock On* album were both released in the UK. The recording of the album wasn't easy, with the film and show to do, plus the demands that fame takes on your time, but although my attention was spread all over the place, it was still fun. Jeff and I used the same musicians and engineer that we used on the first two songs, and with the international success of our first single there was a terrific confidence running through the whole team.

Our wish to experiment and find new sounds was always a trademark of the recordings Jeff and I made. I remember when we recorded 'Lamplight' we booked a man from Leyton to come in and play a blacksmith's anvil on the 'Shine on Me' parts. He duly arrived with his anvil in a canvas bag and various sizes of hammer. Unfortunately this went the same way as the didgeridoo, and I finished up playing a fire extinguisher on it instead.

Christmas was on the way and 'Lamplight' was climbing into the top five. I now had two albums in the album chart – *That'll Be the Day* was still in the top twenty and the *Rock On* album was on the way up. The 'Rock On' single topped charts world-wide and was moving slowly but surely up the American top hundred.

Next I was voted 'The Most Promising Newcomer' by the Royal Variety Club – slightly ironic – but I managed to get to the lunch and say a sincere thank you. Awards were being heaped on me from every quarter. Jeff received a Best Producer thing from the *New Musical Express.* I even received the accolade of 'Rear of the Year'. That one I didn't turn up to collect. Even though I won it, or should I say my rear won it, another three or four times, I still never went up to claim my prize.

I was just looking forward to a quieter Christmas when Derek received a call from the management of The Who, asking if I would be interested in playing Pete Townshend's part in a live concert version of something Pete had written called *Tommy*. I obviously knew Keith Moon, who was going to strut his stuff, so I agreed. We did it with the minimum of rehearsal at the Rainbow, Finsbury Park. I remember the theatre was so cold that the string players were wearing gloves.

Strange to think I was involved in the first live version of *Tommy*, as later, when the film was made, Ken Russell approached me to sing 'Pinball Wizard' in it. I recorded the track at Pete Townsend's studio, but when they made the film Elton John was wangled in. Russell did the same to me years before. I was told verbally I was going to play opposite Twiggy in a film called *The Boyfriend*, and I even attended dance lessons and worked with Twiggy on routines for it. Then, just before the start date, a ballet dancer was cast instead. Mind you, having seen the film, Ken did me a favour.

Talking of films, when I signed to do *That'll Be the Day* I also signed to do a sequel. If the first film was successful, the producers had an option on me to make a follow-up and, as the first film was such a hit, David Puttnam exercised the option. Originally it was to be called *Sooner Or Later*, but the title later changed to *Stardust*.

# 10

# Stardust Memories

It might have been more apt to keep the title 'Sooner Or Later', for after a short Christmas break that the family and I made the best of, I received news that filming for *Stardust* was to begin in February 1974, just a month or so away. Definitely sooner rather than later.

Ray Connolly again had written the script, which followed on from the last scene of *That'll Be the Day*, where the character I played, Jim MacLaine, is seen buying a guitar. *Stardust* continued the story of Jim in a definitive film of the creation, rise and fall of a top Sixties rock superstar through to 1970.

Although the producers and writers were the same, the director was now to be Michael Apted and the part of Mike had passed from Ringo Starr to Adam Faith. Ringo felt he had lived it in real life and didn't want to re-live it in a fictionalized way. As time went on I understood why. So many of the things I was fictionalizing as Jim were happening to Dave in real life that an identity crisis was looming.

In Britain the *Rock On* album went gold and both singles went silver. A quick trip was scheduled to Los Angeles for a *That'll Be the Day* premiere, some American TV and a swift holiday in Mexico before filming was scheduled to start on 4 February.

It was while I was in America that I got the idea for the next single, to be called – guess what – 'America', a kind of musical diary of the people I met and the things I saw. CBS were after a follow-up to 'Lamplight', so Jeff and I quickly went in and put it down. I had to leave Jeff to finish it, as I was soon off on location to start filming *Stardust*.

This film was shot in slightly more exotic locations than the Isle of Wight. This time Spain, America and England would provide the backdrops. It was nice to team up again with some of the folks with whom I'd made *That'll Be the Day*, but the subject-matter was much less fun than the first film.

I enjoyed myself in the early parts of the film which mainly consisted of my character being a band member of the film's group, the Stray Cats, a group which included that other Jesus, Paul Nicholas, as well as Dave Edmunds, Karl Howman, Peter Duncan and Keith Moon.

I think because Ray Connolly, Keith, Adam, Dave and myself had all had first-hand experience of the music business (Ray because he was a writer for the *Liverpool Echo* and had been close to the Liverpool explosion with the Beatles and other bands), we were able to bring a truth to what we were doing.

To film a big concert scene the producers took over Belle Vue in Manchester and invited David Essex fans to the show. Bearing in mind I had not yet toured with my new-found fame, there was much excitement. Belle Vue, a massive venue, was packed.

I remember the first assistant, a great chap called Garth Thomas, trying in vain to get the crowd to shout 'We want Jim', not 'We want David' – but it just didn't happen. When we hit the stage pandemonium broke out, providing brilliant realism for the film-makers and, for me, and a clue of what was to come.

One strange all-night shoot, again at Belle Vue, also sticks in my mind. People were tired and things were dragging on when out of nowhere a fight broke out between Keith and Ray. Well, not so much a fight, more like handbags at ten paces. The make-up man got hysterical and started jumping up and down and pleading, 'Don't hit his face, don't hit his face' – obviously worried about Keith's good looks.

To try and calm things down I persuaded a helpful chap to open the bowling alley for us, which he kindly did. It was about four in the morning as Keith, bowling ball in hand, advanced menacingly to bowl his first ball. I still have this mental picture of Keith, wearing a red velvet jacket, sliding down the alley on his backside, still holding the ball, and disappearing into the ten pin mechanism – and the clearing gate coming down again and again in a vain attempt to clear the obstruction. Finally our helpful friend and I rescued Keith and pulled him out still holding his bowling ball. Keith declared a strike.

Keith also got his roadie to rig up a hidden speaker by the radiator in his car. This was linked to a microphone inside the car. Much fun was had stopping nicely at crossings for pedestrians, and then scaring them with a booming 'Get out of the road!'

After one particular night shoot, Keith and I returned to the Midland Hotel in Manchester where we were staying at about four in the morning. Derek had left a message for me with the reception desk which simply read, 'Congratulations – You're Number One in America.' After a remarkably slow climb up the US charts 'Rock On' had finally reached Number One. I showed the message to Keith, who seemed more excited than me. 'Champagne!' he proclaimed, adding, 'You lucky sod. The Who have never had a number one,' and the drinking commenced.

Keith was a pretty original chap and we miss him.

Filming in Spain was interesting. Adam Faith and I travelled to a semi-derelict castle which was the location for the character's refuge in the film.

Jim MacLaine at the height of his fame decides to become a recluse, so he and Mike, his road manager and Man Friday, played by Adam, buy this remote Moorish castle. The Castillio was near

117

a village called Gaudix, which was very basic. We stayed in what can only be described as a hovel. I remember a distraught Maureen describing how a rat had run across Verity as she lay asleep in bed.

Adam and I must have been deeply into the parts we were playing at the time, because Adam started to make enquiries with regard to buying the place. The main problem seemed to be that upon buying the castle you also bought the troglodytes that lived in the caves below it. I had this mental picture of the villagers up in arms and a torchlight procession storming the castle walls, where only boiling oil could placate their wrath. Thankfully we saw sense and never bought it.

Adam also took me to another place that he was thinking of buying, this time in England. We had a break in filming one afternoon owing to a thunderstorm, with lightning and heavy rain, so Bert, Adam's road manager, who would supply Adam with large quantities of lemon tea, drove us to inspect the place Adam fancied.

After a short trip we turned into a long drive leading to a large Gothic building. As a dramatic thunderclap crashed overhead, Bert pulled the Jaguar up at the front door. What a great place for a horror film, I thought, as we went inside. Adam had brought me to a psychiatric hospital not unlike the one where I had left Michael. Apparently the residents were being moved and the place was for sale.

As we walked in, a gentleman inmate plastered some baked beans over his face as Adam, undeterred, went through the alterations he planned if he bought the place. Throughout the visit, owing to his excitement at the impending purchase, he seemed oblivious to what was going on around us, except for the odd 'Hello' to an inmate who happened to be where the planned snooker room or master bedroom would be.

I liked Adam a lot, but I found it difficult to share his enthusiasm for either venture – although the castle had the weather.

Filming on location in the States was pretty exciting. With 'Rock On' topping their charts, would-be American managers were coming out of the woodwork. This was the kind of thing that made the making of *Stardust* difficult.

So much of the make-believe in the film was being mirrored by me in real life. Just as Larry Hagman (JR in *Dallas*) muscled in and took over my management in the film, US managers were trying on the same persuasive arguments. Thank goodness my East End loyalty stood the test.

When we filmed in Los Angeles, Larry invited us to a party at his Malibu beach house. Larry was almost as good a hell-raiser as any I've met, and a little out of the ordinary. He had this telescope thing in a trailer where he would lie and watch the stars at night, and in his bedroom there was a bed that did many things including vibrating at speed. I remember Keith being cautioned for working the bed too hard. 'You'll break the God-damn thing,' Larry explained, just before most of the guests disappeared naked into the sea.

I found *Stardust* and its subject-matter hard to do, but in some ways what happened to my character, especially in the latter half of the film, helped to signpost a path for me through the pitfalls of drugs and the seduction of fame. If there was ever a time when I was vulnerable, I feel, it was around this period, when, if you like, David Essex almost got lost in an alter ego called Jim MacLaine.

Looking back, I think living the character both on and off the screen, plus the manic schedule, meant that when filming finished and when the adrenaline stopped flowing, exhaustion hit me. I remember visiting my mum and how concerned she was as she surveyed my gaunt face and lack of energy.

The record company were already looking for another album and single and I suspect that it was going back to music, after the break of filming, although pretty whacked, that helped me cope.

Jeff had in the meantime gone to America, recorded the backing vocals using his first choice of vocal groups The Persuasions and had finished 'America'. It was released in May 1974, and although it charted, it never made the top ten in the UK, probably because the lyric was too personal.

This wasn't the case in France, where the song became the biggest foreign hit ever, staying at number one for months. Curious to know why, I asked a French record executive what could be the reason. He told me his theory – the chorus of America goes 'America, America – ca ca', and 'ca ca' is apparently the French equivalent of poo poo. This obviously appealed to the xenophobic French. And I thought it was just a catchy song...

Talking of France, Maureen, Verity and I have spent a fair deal of time in the South of France, which is one of my favourite places. One time when we were there I met up with my good friend Kenney Jones, the ex-drummer of the Small Faces and ironically Keith Moon's replacement in The Who. One night, Kenney and I went out for a drink in a club in St Tropez where we got roped in to judge a beauty contest. My time as a judge though was short-lived as, seeing the funny side of proceedings, I gave my marks in fractions. As the totals were read out to the crowd they were greeted with muted laughter as Miss St Maxime, for instance, received thirty-nine and three-eighths!

After being relieved of our duties, Kenney and I decided to head back to the villa I'd rented next door to Jean-Michel Jarre, but not before relieving ourselves against a wall in a nearby street. There I was quietly answering the call of nature, when from out of nowhere an arm went round my neck and I was dragged away – still with my flies wide open and swaying in the breeze.

My mistake seems to have been that the wall selected belonged to the police station. Once inside, with my flies safely done up, I was quizzed and rebuked until one burly policeman recognized

A cold morning on the set of *Stardust*. Left to right: Bedford Dormobile group van,
Keith Moon, me, Karl Howman, Paul Nicholas and Dave Edmunds.

The Stray Cats run through a tune called *You Keep Me Waiting* prior to recording.

Cher and me on Cher's show in LA. I
can't remember the duet, but I remember
doing a comedy sketch with Jerry Lewis
on the show.

*Left:* Photos from this Brian Aris session
were used around the time of *America*.

*Right:* Looking "cool" on the front cover of a teen mag.

*Below:* Getting in unscathed for a concert.

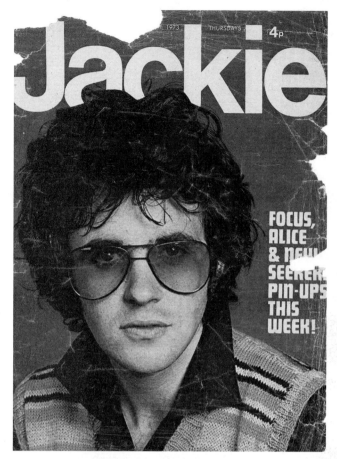

*Above:* An electric shock of love on a UK tour in the middle Seventies. *Left:* A rose between two bushes: Bev on my right and Mel on my left somewhere on a concert tour in the middle Seventies.

*Opposite page, top:* A "Bad Taste Party" that Maureen and I threw on top of a pub in East London – that's me with the wonky sunglasses and the dodgy moustache with Jeremy Irons looking rather dashing to my right. *Below:* Later that night, me, Denny Laine and Mike Batt decide to rock!

*Opposite page, top:* Recording *War of the Worlds* in LA with Richard Burton. From left to right: Sharon Weiz, Richard Burton, Jerry Wayne, Jeff Wayne and the Artillery Man … me!

*Below:* Scruff the dog and me at home in Chigwell, a stone's throw from Bobby Moore's house. The jukebox was a present from the film *Stardust*, the wallpaper very Seventies.

*This page, top:* Me as Che in *Evita*, taken just before our opening in London.

*Right:* Elaine (Evita) Paige and me at some award shindig.

*Above:* Having just been assembled at Silverstone, me and the Silver Dream Machine take off, much to the horror of the film producers. *Right:* Beau Bridges and me. He never rode bikes, but he was still OK.

me: 'Daveed Esseex – America – ca ca.' He then brokered a deal – I would be let off from a night in a police cell if I gave them a rendition of 'America'. Faced with little choice, I climbed up on to the table and sang it. It felt like some strange initiation ceremony for the Foreign Legion. Kenney could hardly keep a straight face as the local constabulary joined in. It was an unusual end to an unusual evening, as we bade our backing group goodbye and made it back to the villa, wives and kids.

It was in the South of France that I wrote most of the second album, *David Essex*. I had invited my promotion man Steve Collier over for a holiday. Steve was a terrific worker on my behalf and helped a great deal with air play and television around my record releases. Steve also is an artiste and writer in his own right and for good measure had brought along his guitar. I remember one lunchtime by the pool, as he was playing a sequence of chords, a tune popped into my head which in time turned out be a number one in Britain – 'Gonna Make You a Star'. I'd like to thank Steve for that. When the single earned a Gold Disc, he was the first one to get a copy. Steve still remains a close friend today.

With the *Stardust* film due for release in the autumn of 1974, I decided to write a song for the film soundtrack, to be called 'Stardust'. This time, David Puttnam put it straight into the film and it played as the credits rolled. I have one vivid memory of recording that song. We were trying to find a searing, falling sound to put behind the vocal where I sing 'In a stardust ring see the rock'n'roll king is down.' We tried some synthesizer sounds, then a detuned bass, and finally Ray Cooper the magical percussionist came up with the idea of filling a small bath with water, hitting a gong and dropping it into the water: as the gong submerged, the pitch of the note dropped. It was a brilliant sound and it made it to the record, but we did flood the studio.

Jeff and I got on with recording the rest of the songs I'd written, and Derek started to talk to promoters with regard to what seemed to be an eagerly awaited autumn tour. He narrowed down the number of promoters he thought he could trust to a short list of two, and we then met with them both.

The second one we met we liked immediately. A country boy called Mel Bush, he seemed honest, down to earth, and enthusiastic. Together we decided to do fifteen dates in major cities in November. (It was the start of a wonderful and trusting relationship with Mel and his family that has lasted till today. Ann and Mel's other sisters have been a great help over the years.) The tour would coincide with the release of the album (*David Essex*), the film (*Stardust*) and the film soundtrack album – again we could conquer the world!

But first we needed to prepare for the rock tour.

# 11

# Essex Mania

Jeff, although brilliant in the studio, had limited experience in live work. Now, because of some of the unusual sounds on our record-ings, he had to work out a line-up of musicians that could repro-duce live the sound and arrangements we had on the records. He did this very successfully. It was quite a large line-up, about nine musicians as I recall, plus three backing singers.

These were heady times as we rehearsed selected songs from the two albums that would constitute the set. The single 'Stardust', my album and the film album were all climbing the charts. The film was massive and the tour had sold out within two days of tickets going on sale. I expected a warm reception, but I was quite unprepared for what happened.

We had rehearsed the show and the band was sounding great. Now the big day had arrived. Nervously, I ran through some songs at the sound-check, before my first show at the Odeon, East Ham – not three miles from where I was born. I reflected how far Derek and I had come, and that it felt right to open the tour in my local rock venue. At one time there had been approaches to tour the US first, but I always wanted to start at home.

As I sat in the dressing-room after the final sound-check I could hear the crowds beginning to form outside. I was on my own. Even today before a show my dressing-room is never full of people. It's a time when I prefer to be alone and focus.

Mel's brother Bev was my road manager, a wonderful friend who lived and worked with me for many years after. Bev quickly got to know me and made sure I had some time by myself. This first night was a little eerie. Even though I knew I was surrounded by so much love, I felt lonely. It's a feeling I still get today when I tour: you share so much with your audience and then finish up in a hotel room alone.

Bev tapped his secret knock on the door and said, 'They're ready when you are.'

'I'm ready,' I said, put on my jacket and made for the stage. A roaring scream erupted as Jeff and the band kicked off. When I made my entrance the volume of the music and the screaming was unbelievable. It seemed as if everything had gone into slow motion. Above me, to the left, I saw what looked like a shadow coming towards me. It turned out to be a girl who had dived headlong out of the royal box and landed in a heap at my feet. Never having faced this before, I thought the best thing to do was to move to another part of the stage and hope that the security people would carry her off. I'm pleased to say she wasn't hurt and even made another attempt to get to me later.

After all our meticulous work on putting together a top band, on the night you could hardly hear us and we could hardly hear each other. The audience was incredible, and the love I felt was almost overwhelming. Audiences have given me so much over the years, for which I thank them, and I will never take that warmth for granted.

The show itself was relatively easy compared with getting out of the theatre; every exit was blocked by thousands of fans. Bev, with the aid of security men, devised a way out, over the roofs, into another building and out to a waiting car by a service entrance – I felt as if I'd joined the SAS. We made it through unscathed, and

I signed a few autographs for a handful of fans who had cracked the getaway plot.

I've had some eventful getaways over the years, none more so than when I did two shows at the Liverpool Empire, more or less back to back. The sell-out audience from the first show decided to stay in the streets surrounding the theatre to hear the second show, which meant that, when we were ready to leave, there were about six thousand people surrounding the place and it was impossible to get out.

Police roamed the area with dogs, trying to restore order as the centre of Liverpool was brought to a standstill. After discussions with the superintendent in charge, a plan was hatched. I was to be dressed in a police uniform, and at a selected exit the nine or ten policemen surrounding me would burst out of the exit as if it was a skirmish, put me in a police car and, with a police escort, get me back to the relative safety of the Adelphi Hotel. With only a few misgivings I changed into an ill-fitting uniform and we assembled by our getaway door. It might well have worked, but the problem was that I had no boots to change into. I still wore some rather dashing red boots, so as the exit door flew open and the fabricated skirmish hit the street, we were twigged immediately. At least five coppers were up-ended, and if it hadn't been for the quick thinking of a burly sergeant, who put me over his shoulder, used me as a battering ram and dumped me in the back of a police Land Rover, I might never have made it. As it was, we had to spend most of the night in the police station till the crowd dispersed in the early hours of the morning.

Another time, when I was due to do an interview at Radio One, DJ Tony Blackburn had trailered the fact that I was coming in to do it live. We were just about to leave for the interview when my promotion man at the time, a chap called Colin, received a call warning us that a massive crowd had gathered outside Broadcasting House waiting to see me. Colin had an idea.

I had a blacked-out Mini that I would occasionally use, so Colin's brainwave was for me to go with Bev in the Mini while he travelled in the limo with a cardboard cut-out of me. The fans would be attracted to the limo and my cardboard cut-out while Bev and I could get out of the Mini and into the radio station without much bother.

The amazing thing is that we agreed to do it. We travelled in convoy to Broadcasting House, and when we turned into Portland Place there were thousands there. The limo went ahead as planned to draw the crowd, but all it drew was a puzzled indifference. When the Mini was seen all hell broke loose, cries of 'There he is!' filled the air, and in no time at all we were surrounded. It was scary, there were so many girls on top of the car that we thought the roof would give way. The weight broke the back springs. Bev was panicking, which was very unusual. He said 'Stay here' – as if I had an option – 'I'll go for help' and he forced his way out of the car. Now it's an odd sensation to be surrounded and engulfed in a little car with about twenty hysterical faces crushed and pressed against the window, with a few hundred behind waiting to take their place. You don't quite know how to react. Do you wave? Do you tell them to get off the car? Do you smile or look angry? – I had no idea, and as one black girl pressed her face to the windscreen and said, 'You know why, don't you? Cos we fucking love ya,' the best I could do was look sheepish and try to smile.

Bev the warrior fought his way back to me and the car with news from the front. When he went into the foyer and asked the Commissionaires for help they responded with, 'Don't you bring him in here.' Thanks I thought, but Bev reassured me that the police were on their way. By the time we were rescued half the West End had ground to a halt.

I've also had some moments when girls have come out of wardrobes in hotel rooms or materialized in dressing-rooms. I've even had two young girls climb in through my bedroom window.

The strange thing is that generally, when confronted by the person they want to see the realization of what they've done hits them and they become nervous and sorry. Sometimes, however, they're on a mission and then it's a little worrying.

One of the weirdest things I have found when touring, especially in the Seventies and Eighties, is the sudden change of mood after doing a show. You run the gauntlet to get out of the venue, there's usually a mad car chase to beat the fans back to the hotel, and then it's quickly into a lift and back to an empty room. It's a strange sensation, and my ears would ring for hours from the volume of screaming. I'd be locked away and, although so much love seemed to be surrounding me, there I was, sitting in a quiet hotel room, purposefully cut off from the outside world.

Being cut off from the outside world is something I have always tried to avoid. I've seen quite a few famous folk surround themselves with an impregnable entourage, only for the entourage to become the only outside world the famous one knows. A dangerous situation, as yes-men only say yes.

With a phenomenal first tour over, it seemed I was now Britain's biggest performing artiste in every popular medium, but, even knowing this, thankfully, my feet were still pretty near to the ground. I'm sure what helped me not to believe the fantasy, and to maintain a hold on reality, were the many years Derek and I battled against the odds, when the only one who really believed in me was Derek. Equally helpful were my family, my concern that my daughter should respect her dad, and of course the knowledge in the back of my mind that before my fame, when I was invisible, I was exactly the same person as the larger-than-life figure I had become. Why should someone as lucky as me, who is able to work at something he loves, feel more worthy than anyone else? I certainly never have. Like that Hans Christian Anderson story where the ugly duckling becomes a swan, it seemed I had become a swan but I still remembered being an ugly duckling.

# 12

# All the Fun of the Fair

After the first two hit albums I started to think about that all-important third album and began putting down some ideas, but before I could develop them a US tour was put together. The record company in America had frankly been annoyed at my schedule in Europe and seized upon a time window to get me across to America.

Jeff and the band flew out with me for a mixture of showcase shows and concerts, the first being at the famous Bottom Line in New York. It was exciting to be in New York, a city I love. A few years later, I bought a loft there and spent a good deal of time in the city of cities.

One particular concert I remember was in St Louis, where I topped the bill and the band Journey were support. The stadium was massive, and 28,000 people were there. Journey were supposed to go on and do a set lasting an hour, but after an hour and twenty minutes, they were still at it. It was at this point that Derek actually walked over and pulled the mains plug. It all went dark and very quiet except for the disgruntled grunts of Journey and their entourage creeping off in the darkness. We finally went on, and surprisingly the audience were still there.

When we were down in Georgia, a guitarist of mine, who shall remain nameless, committed the cardinal sin it seems of peeing in the hotel ice-making machine. The local sheriff was called, and the boys and I had to make a run for it into the woods behind the hotel with shots being fired over our heads.

There was one very strange night when I played the Roxy in Los Angeles and Led Zeppelin came to watch. After the show we met up for a drink and they were telling me about some FBI agents that were guarding their apartments in the wake of the Charles Manson murders. We said goodnight and I went back to the Beverly Wiltshire Hotel where the family and I were staying.

With thoughts of murder and things floating through my brain I started to drift off when I saw the shape of a head at the end of our bed. 'Verity?' I said. Then from the shape came an unearthly grunt followed by Maureen's bag hitting me in the face. The shape left the room, then things gradually turned into a black comedy film. I was naked and determined that I was not going to face this murderous sect in my birthday suit. I fumbled for a pair of jeans, but only succeeded in getting stuck in a pair of Maureen's and banging my toe in the process. Eventually, with my jeans on, I hurried to the bedroom of Verity and our new nanny, Shirley. After they had assured me they were OK I prepared to meet my doom in the suite's lounge. Nervously I opened the door – it was empty, no people chanting and waving knives about – empty. The telephone rang, I jumped. It was the LA police in the lobby saying they had already apprehended two suspects running down a fire escape from our room.

Then it got really silly. First the police took me down to a police car to identify them. How could I if I hadn't seen them? I made an effort, though, and as I looked into the car, one of the inmates spat on the window. Nice chap, I thought. Next, a cop tried to plant heroin on me, presumably because I was a rock star. Then I was left with a psychopath in LAPD uniform to search the hotel for our stolen cash and credit cards.

Rambo and I stopped on every one of the hotel's many floors.

The lift door would open, he'd go out first with his gun drawn, then give me a nod if the coast was clear. We would then search the corridors and sand buckets for what seemed much longer than I was interested. 'Not to worry,' I'd say, in the hope that he'd give up, but no, this guy was serious. After what seemed like hours we found nothing – but then again we didn't search the policemen.

Apart from a few frustrations, the US tour went well. It was the only time I toured America, I'm not sure why. I suppose I just preferred being in England, but also it seemed I was always involved in projects here. It was a path that probably led to the US record company in time losing interest in me.

Back home again I started writing songs for the third album. In fact one song, which turned out to be 'Hold Me Close', came to me in Los Angeles. For the writing of this album I was able to concentrate in a more sustained way without the distraction of working on a film or stage show. The writing was only disturbed by the odd television or press commitment.

When I was thirteen or so I had worked in the school holidays on a visiting fun-fair. I was fascinated by the travelling lifestyle and the underlying smell of violence that you felt was just a whiff away from the candy floss, the merry-go-round, good times and flashing lights.

It was good to mix with the showmen again when filming *That'll Be the Day*, so I suppose it was pretty logical for me to come up with a song – and an album – called 'All the Fun of the Fair' by way of a tribute. We had had three hit singles from the *David Essex* album, so CBS were looking to repeat the success by releasing one or two singles up front from the forthcoming album.

Jeff and I got to work quickly. Recording the *All the Fun of the Fair* album was great, as Jeff and I seemed really in tune. Some of the arrangements he did for my songs were terrific. The engineer who had worked with us on 'Rock On', Gary Martin, had left studio work and headed off to the Welsh hills to concentrate on making Medieval musical instruments, and was replaced by another talented engineer named Geoff Young. We used a mix of musicians, of whom some had played on my first recordings and others had been with me for the live work. I think the fact that we had toured, lived and played concerts together, brought a closer understanding to the recording process. We had also started working with the Real Thing, who were terrific. I loved their voices and attitude in the studio, and the backing vocals they contributed to the album provided a valuable backdrop to the sound of it.

Because we were having such a good time we went past our deadline to finish the album, and consequently we were being harassed by impatient record executives, flown in from all over the world and anxious for a playback.

We were so up against it that I was still doing the last vocal for the album, the one for 'Hold Me Close', as the hierarchy from the record company sat in the studio reception, having been herded in by Derek. Two vocal takes, a quick half an hour mix and bosh! It turned out to be one of my biggest records. After a wait of an hour and a half the record people were let in, we offered our apologies and Jeff pushed the play button.

I've found it very interesting to watch people at these kind of playbacks. You are looking for a reaction, of course, but the reactions of record company folk, I've found, seem to depend entirely on the big cheese – the top bloke. The more positively he reacts, the more positively the entourage reacts. It's a bit like being an A and R man: you keep your job longer if you don't sign an act, because if you actually sign one and they don't sell records, you get the sack. It's strange, the world of record companies.

After listening through, the big cheese's reaction was good, so the compliments started to flow, release dates were discussed, singles were singled out, and copies were taken away.

Although over the years Jeff and I listened to the good and bad ideas of the record company, musically we always made the final decisions between ourselves. So when we wanted a particular single the company agreed, probably because of the success of the unusual 'Rock On'. This time, a little against their wishes, we put out 'Rolling Stone' as the first single. Thankfully it was another hit, and our record on records remained unblemished.

It was the summer of 1975, and Derek, Mel Bush and I started to talk of an autumn tour, staged around the *All the Fun of the Fair* album. It was an emotive image to develop. I suggested the straightforward concept of using a fun-fair as a stage set, so work began on a Big Wheel. This tour turned out to be a far-reaching outing into many other countries. We played in front of fanatical audiences in Europe and Scandinavia (I wonder if Beth came?), rocking audiences in Australia, and some odd audiences in Germany. It was almost a world tour.

This was the tour that probably sealed our worth as a live act in Britain. Audiences were starting to listen to and really hear the wonderful musicians we had assembled. In London we did a week at the famous rock venue the Hammersmith Odeon, and to celebrate Mel had this enormous billboard painted of me and hung up, covering the whole front of the theatre. He was ordered to take it down the next day as Hammersmith council said it was a danger to drivers crossing the Hammersmith flyover. One glimpse of a giant David Essex coming towards them might cause them to crash. The long and expansive tour was great. It was good to visit so many places, even if it was in a slightly superficial way.

I especially enjoyed Australia, and above all one magical night in Adelaide when we played an outdoor tennis stadium. It was a wonderful summer night with a crowd stretching as far as the eye could see and thousands listening outside. My bass player on the tour Mike Thorn whispered in my ear, 'Is this a dream or is this real?' Whatever it was, the tour was remarkable.

Australia and Australians I like very much. If you've just spent time in LA it is particularly refreshing to go to Australia, where people are straightforward and there is none of that superficiality that engulfs you in LA. I had the good fortune of touring Australia again just recently with Tim Rice on a tour featuring his songs, backed by a large orchestra and with INXS as our rhythm section. I really enjoyed it. For a change, too, I was able to see some of the country as we played each city for a week or so.

On reflection 1975 was a busy year. I produced my friend Steve Collier and a single with The Real Thing, and both were terrific when they appeared with me in front of 18,000 people on a wonderful night at Earls Court. The next single, released in September, was that rush job 'Hold Me Close', followed by the *All the Fun of the Fair* album. Both were big records, and I still get the odd builder giving me a rendition of 'Hold Me Close' as I walk past a building site.

After all the amazing solo success, when the tour finished I must have subconsciously wanted to dissolve inside a band again, because I was trying to feature my band much more.

The personnel had changed. Jeff was no longer touring with us but the musicians I had then and have had playing for me over the years are an impressive bunch: people like Mark Griffiths who left to fulfil his boyhood dream to play with the Shadows and still does to this day; Andy Summers, who went on to conquer the world with Police; Mike Thorn, who played that brilliant 'City Lights' bass riff; Phil Palmer, who now plays alongside a friend of mine, Eric Clapton; the brilliant Alan Wakeman, the legend Herbie Flowers – the list is endless. I'm sure that being able to attract brilliant musicians, right up to the excellent band I have today, has helped in a big way to establish me as a live performer. The brotherhood and shared sense of humour certainly kept me almost sane.

In this band frame of mind I approached the next album in a

different way, thinking of it less as a solo singer's album than as a band piece. For the first time there was a hint of an artistic rift between Jeff Wayne and me. As we routined the album I was keen to use the same musicians I had been using on the road and wanted the album to sound like that of a band. Jeff thought this would limit us, and he may have been right, but I got my way and we started recording *Out on the Street* after the extensive tour in 1976.

I may have been singing about the city, but the family and I had bought a farm in Kent and spent as much time there as possible. Verity would dress up and entertain the cows with her singing. They were an attentive audience as Verity gave them renditions of current pop songs with Scruff the dog by her side attempting to harmonize.

Scruff was a character. Maureen and I bought him down Petticoat Lane a couple of years before. He was tied to a market stall by a piece of string. Having just outgrown the puppy stage, he was not as cuddly as the puppies on the stall, and seemed to be ignored by would-be buyers. When I asked the stall-holder how much he was, he replied ten pounds, informing me that Scruff's vaccinations had cost five pounds! We bought him and were given some kind of pedigree certificate saying that Maximilian was something or other, which was strange as Max was definitely a classic mongrel. How proud he was as we led him away on his bit of string – his front paws never touched the ground. It seemed that Max, now rightly named Scruff, had read the dog handbook: he would go for postmen's ankles, terrorize the dustmen, pick fights with dogs twice his size and occasionally go missing, turning up at various police stations with his tail between his legs.

He also had a fairly new friend, a film star. If you remember, in *Stardust* my character cruelly gives Mike's dog an LSD tablet. In real life, I had gotten very fond of Rover, the dog in the film. Because of the quarantine regulations in Britain, the producers were going to leave Rover in Spain, but I decided to pay for him to come back, and after his spell in prison he spent many happy times down on the farm being nipped and chased by Scruff the nutter. They became good friends and were a comical duo, a little mongrel and a very big Airedale terrier, but of course Scruff was the boss. It was touching later, when Scruff got old and his eyes and ears went, how Rover used to take care of him and try to keep him out of mischief.

That summer of 1976 was a beautiful one, and felt like one long picnic, as the smell of honeysuckle filled the air. It was good to have some time off. I was as big as I could be, so Derek and I had begun saying no to things – not only to give me a break, but also to give the poor public some time away from David Essex.

Meanwhile, in the outside world, punk had come into fashion, which I liked and welcomed. I marvelled from a distance at the hysteria of the media as it built so-called anti-stars into stars. I watched as record companies, in a frenzy, tried to sign anyone that could plug in a guitar. It was good meeting some of the punk bands, while doing a TV show or something. Most had mastered the expected level of yob, but would meekly ask for an autograph in a quiet moment.

When it came to releasing *Out on the Street* at this time, it was a plus really that I'd decided to come up with a more hard-edged sound. It wasn't the happiest of recordings, but still it has some interesting moments.

'City Lights' was the first single, I think, and although it made the top thirty it wasn't a massive hit, probably because it was over five minutes long. It suffered through lack of air play. But hearing Paul McCartney sing it to me in an Italian restaurant with Linda was cool.

The Real Thing and I filmed a video for 'City Lights', using the East End streets as a backdrop, but because of the chart position the video just failed to find a spot on the very important *Top of the Pops* and lost its momentum.

I played a week at the London Palladium that year and although there were no bears this time, I had a circus with me – tigers, the lot. I had also seen a dance group called Hot Gossip in a club and booked them through their choreographer Arlene Phillips, whom I first met doing those tap lessons for *The Boyfriend*.

The show was bonkers, and the llama would always poop on the stage. The whiff of llama poo as I sang 'If I Could' sort of shattered the mood. Still, it was nice to come back to the Palladium, and this time to emerge from the shadows.

I also did a few TV shows in America about this time, including *The Johnny Carson Show* and *The Cher Show*. Cher was fine, but I had to do this comedy sketch with Jerry Lewis, with me dressed as a cowboy. It was lousy. I much prefer Norman Wisdom.

Although I was still doing lots of things, the less than manic pace of it all was most welcome. *Out on the Street* came out in late '76 and did OK, but the singles 'Coming Home' and 'Ooh Love' never made the top ten. I think this probably created a little tension between Jeff and me, and although we remained good friends, and still are today, I was now looking to produce myself.

Producing yourself, as I have done many times since, is not the easiest path to take, especially when recording your own vocals. I found I would spend hours getting a drum sound right and treat the lead vocals as an afterthought. Objectivity is difficult to maintain, but the good thing is that, for better or worse, you are in control.

Jeff let go of his producer role, and I worked more closely with the band, especially my guitarist at the time, Mark Griffiths. This probably suited Jeff, as he asked me what I thought about him writing and recording a musical version of H.G. Wells's *The War of the Worlds*. I told him I thought it was a good idea, and he went away and got on with his own epic while I prepared, in the spring of 1977, to write and produce *Gold and Ivory*.

This album was to be my fifth and final album under my recording contract with both Jeff Wayne Music and CBS Records, and I was very keen to finish on a high note by coming up with a strong last album.

For the recording I decided to get out of London and leave the familiar Advision Studio for the Manor Studios in Oxfordshire. The Manor was owned by Richard Branson and was a decent studio with accommodation, in which the band and I stayed. It meant I could record any time of the night and day, plus the musicians were always at hand. It was, I felt, a very creative way of recording, but not cheap.

The Manor, as the name suggests, was in fact a very old building, reputed to house a mysterious ghost. Ronnie Leahy, my keyboard player, was convinced the place was haunted. I was not convinced until one early morning after a long night in the studio when I'd bid the band goodnight and gone to bed about 2.30 a.m. I'd just fallen asleep when something woke me. Clearing my eyes, I looked towards the fireplace and saw a grey figure of a man dressed in seventeenth-century clothes, warming himself by an imaginary fire.

Now I don't know if you've ever seen a ghost and, if you have, how you reacted, but it didn't freak me out at all. I calmly watched my room-mate with interest, as he stood with his back to me, rubbing his shadowy hands together by an open grate. Then, after two or three minutes, he seemed to dissolve, leaving me to wonder if I'd really seen him at all.

The next morning, at breakfast, I related my haunting to the staff and the band. The girls serving breakfast confirmed that the chap I'd seen was indeed a regular visitor. Spooky.

I tried hard to make the material for the album as strong as possible and wrote two or three songs with my old mate Steve Collier. The other nine I routined and rehearsed with the band – Barry DeSouza on drums; Mark Griffiths, bass; Ronnie Leahy, keyboards; Phil Palmer, guitar; and Alan Wakeman, saxophones.

I enjoyed the responsibility of producing it and had fun recording the drums, especially sometimes using only room mikes, which made every hit of the drum sound like a bomb going off.

*Gold and Ivory* was a joy to make and remains many people's favourite of all my albums.

# 13

# Do I Want to be Elvis?

CBS were only too aware that my contract was up and because of our world-wide record success were naturally interested in re-signing me. They even got the champion bike racer Barry Sheene to present me with a Yamaha 250cc off-road bike to sweeten me up.

Talks began between Derek and Mel Bush, who had now become my co-manager, and the heads of CBS. By the time I got to hear of the deal points, they were into million-dollar advances, which for that time and even for today is an enormous deal.

A big meeting was scheduled to go over the final points with a view to me re-signing for another five-album deal. All the top executives, lawyers and accountants flew in from America, and I had a formidable entourage representing me.

I'll never forget that meeting, held in CBS's newly acquired Soho Square offices (which, by the way, I'd probably paid for). From twelve noon till well into the afternoon negotiations rambled on. My group would leave the room to discuss points, as would the record company people. Slowly but surely the two sides were finding common ground. As most points were relevant to me but not too worrying, I went along with my advisers' advice. With both sides in agreement, a final read-through of the proposed contract was begun. All was going well until a clause was read out which I interpreted to mean that CBS, or rather Columbia Records in the UK, had creative control.

Naturally I questioned this, and the response from the Americans was that they intended to make me bigger than Elvis was in the States, but to do that they had to have creative control. I immediately voiced my concern and withdrew to an adjoining boardroom with my advisers. The feeling from my team was that the deal was so big that I should sign it and chip away at the creative control stumbling block later.

We went back to the meeting, where I was fully expected to sign. As the contract was handed to me for signature, I looked up and quietly said, 'I can't sign this.'

The looks around the room were ones of disbelief. 'I can't sell my soul,' I explained. This last worthy statement might just as well have been in Chinese, as no one seemed to understand it. And with 'I have to go. I have a plane to catch,' I left all and sundry bemused and bewildered and headed off to the South of France, reflecting on those startled faces but feeling I'd made the right decision.

When the dust settled, Jeff called me and asked if I was interested in working with him on *War of the Worlds*. He told me that Richard Burton was to narrate it and my friend from *Godspell* Julie Covington was to sing on it too. I now had been away from anything filmic or theatrical for a few years, so the concept album idea appealed to me.

I flew back to England and back into Advision studios. I was very impressed with Jeff's melodies and arrangements and enjoyed singing the part of the Artillery Man. Gary Osborne had done a fine job with the lyrics, and the dialogue, adapted from the book by Jeff's father Jerry and his new wife Doreen, told the story well.

As I had scenes with Richard Burton, Jeff and I flew out to LA, where Richard was filming, to record them with him. I remember reading Richard's bits for Jeff in London, so he could time the scored music to go under the dialogue. Jeff then meticulously edited and cut the music to suit. After a few false starts due to filming commitments, Richard finally made it to the recording studio in central LA. Everything was prepared for the great man. As time was short when Richard arrived, Jeff explained that he had prepared the underscored music for his speeches, both for atmosphere and to let him know the time of each piece. Jeff's face was a picture as Richard replied in that special voice, 'No music, thank you. I'll just read it' – which he did, beautifully.

After that Richard became a friend and led a standing ovation for me when I played the poet Byron in *Childe Byron* at the Young Vic in London. It would have been a privilege to work with the great man again. I loved the theatrical stories he told me. One story I remember was from a time when he was doing a Shakespeare season in Stratford-upon-Avon. It was that wonderful Welsh actor Hugh Griffith's birthday, and the chaps had been supping ale since lunch time, vast volumes of it. In this production, Richard had to wear chain mail, and it was difficult to get on and very difficult to get off. After a lengthy time on stage he felt this mixture of both relief and horror as, bursting for a pee, he just had to let go. A warm tingling sensation ran down his legs and on to the stage below unbeknown to the audience. Sadly, Sir Michael Redgrave followed the secret deluge on to the stage to deliver a soliloquy – in bare feet. Apparently Sir Michael never forgave him.

*War of the Worlds* came out in 1978 and proved what a tremendous talent Jeff was. Richard said he was as pleased with the platinum disc he was awarded as he would have been with an Oscar. Over the years there has been talk of doing a stage version, but sadly as yet it hasn't happened.

# 14

# Oh What a Circus

*War of the Worlds*, or 'War of the Worms' as Herbie Flowers called it, had whetted my appetite for a move back to theatre and as luck would have it my office got a call with regard to a new musical by Tim Rice and Andrew Lloyd Webber called *Evita*.

Now Julie Covington had already had a hit with 'Don't Cry for Me Argentina', and the concept album was in the charts. This meant that there was already interest in the show, so I was very interested. I went in to meet the director, Hal Prince, who had an impressive track record as a big Broadway producer. We shook hands, we talked awhile, and he asked me to sing. I sang 'I Think I'm Going Out Of My Head' and then he asked me to play Che.

A strange choice of song, you may think, but at home things were not going too well between Maureen and me, so in a way I *was* going out of my head. To this day, and it's over twenty years ago, I'm not sure what went wrong between us, we just seemed to argue too much. It's a tribute to the true enduring love and respect we felt for each other that we remain close friends today. Back then we decided to spend more time apart from each other. This hurt, and not seeing Verity so much was very hard.

I tried to concentrate on the show. Rehearsals for *Evita* began in the beginning of May 1978 a long stone's throw from The Roundhouse near Regents Park. As with most musicals, things were added, things were cut. As the old saying goes 'musicals are not written, they're re-written.' Tim, Andrew and Hal seemed to be worried about the fact that Che was younger than the Perons and wouldn't have been around when they were in power. They had this notion of playing him as a student. My point was that the power of Che was partly the look, the bedroom poster, the romantic image of a revolutionary in battle fatigues, and they finally agreed.

As we came closer to our opening night, tempers became short, and there were quite a few tantrums, but I seemed to waltz through it. Hal hardly directed me. I would wander on stage, do my bit to bring about the fall of the Perons, and wander off. It's strange to see later after you've left a show and created the character, how the moves you did either instinctively or for a personal reason become stage directions, and how those that take over slavishly follow them. Hal seemed to work with and direct Elaine Paige and Joss Ackland quite a lot. The only thing I remember him saying to me was 'You are marvellous when you're angry' as I wandered in and out of the show like an outsider.

The first previews at the Prince Edward Theatre were upon us, and media interest was reaching fever pitch. The audience reaction was tremendous. On opening night the applause at the end of the show went on for what seemed like hours. It was a big hit and a star was born – Elaine Paige. Elaine, Joss and I, although respectful of each other, were not close. I suspect the fact that in the musical Che was opposed to their characters had something to do with it: we kept our distance, which probably gave an edge to our performances.

With the cast album high in the charts both here and in America, and me still without a record contract, Derek and Mel started talking seriously to Phonogram Records. A deal was put together, and with no creative control for the record company this time, although Phonogram did suggest, as the show was such a hit, that I should record a single from the show. I thought it was a good idea and they suggested Mike Batt to produce it, so in due course Mike and I went in and recorded 'Oh What a Circus' and another of Che's songs, 'High Flying Adored'. Mike did a brilliant job and the single was a smash. During my six months doing *Evita* I had a very busy dressing-room, as it seemed as if everyone came to see the show and wanted to congratulate me after – Cary Grant, Katharine Hepburn, Ingrid Bergman, Bob Dylan, George Cukor and John Travolta, among others. I remember Princess Margaret saying to me, 'What's good about your part is you're not on all the time', and I kind of agreed. Then she went on to say to Elaine, 'It must be awful dying every night.' It was a wonderful experience to be part of what's thought of as a landmark in British musicals.

I only appeared as Che in the original show. Although Elaine and I were asked to open the show in New York, we were both let down by a mist of lame excuses and the honour was given to Americans.

I was also scheduled to do the *Evita* film a few years later and indeed signed a contract to do it. Oliver Stone, one of the first directors attached to the film, invited me to a meeting in LA and talked about the style of the film, but then the director changed, and changed again. Finally it was Alan Parker who directed the film, and he cast Antonio Banderas. I was flattered to learn that Antonio took my original recordings to learn from. Although I thought Alan Parker did a poor job with the film adaptation, I did think Madonna did well. When I was in the running I had suggested Annie Lennox.

I collected a clutch of awards for the show and really had a good time doing it, except for one week when I had German measles. The *Daily Mail* warned any pregnant readers who were going to *Evita* to sit at the back of the circle. I did my final performance as Che on 4 November 1978, and although it was the day before fireworks night I must have gone out with a bang, as tickets to see me in my last show were going for £500 on the black market.

Although I was showered with awards at this time, Maureen awarded me the greatest prize – a baby boy. We named him Dan. He was and is wonderful, and his birth seemed to bring Maureen and I closer together. So much so that after a serious night out with the boys to wet the baby's head, I returned without sleep to Queen Charlotte's Hospital, where Dan was born, moved Maureen over, got into the bed fully clothed, and slept it off. I was gently reprimanded by the Ward Sister.

# 15

# Wizards and Silver Dreams

Towards the end of *Evita* I was approached to do a film with a motor-cycle racing background, and to write the score for it. I'd had a few offers on the film front, including *The Stud* with Joan Collins, but nothing had really appealed to me. But this idea of a woman loving a man and supporting him in a dream that might well kill him, and of course the chance to cane bikes round some of Britain's legendary racecourses, was too good to miss. I agreed to do the film *Silver Dream Racer*, but first I felt I needed to get back into the studio to record an album for my new company. David Wickes, the director and writer, agreed to wait for me, so off I went to write some songs.

The new album was called *Imperial Wizard*. It became a slightly choppy album to make, as I produced five tracks, Mike Batt three and Chris Neil two. The musicians I managed to get for the recording were brilliant. I had Kenney Jones on drums, Ray Cooper on percussion, Chris Spedding and Phil Palmer on guitars, Francis Monkman on keyboards and Alan Wakeman on saxophones, plus the London Philharmonic.

Even though there was a lack of continuity, the track 'Imperial Wizard' and the album itself are among the recordings I'm really proud of. The single 'Imperial Wizard' was prevented from being a top ten hit, I believe, by a snowstorm that held up the chart returns for two weeks. Standing still in the chart at number thirty-one meant it lost its momentum.

On the album I loved working with the Scottish folk group the Whistlebinkies. I had written a kind of folk song entitled, 'Are You Still My True Love' and wanted to use some authentic folk instruments for the recording. I like the Irish Chieftains a lot and in my search for a similar line-up came across the Whistlebinkies. The problem was that my engineer wasn't sure how to mike up some of the instruments, some of which he'd never seen before. Eventually we got going and had a right old knees-up, they were very Scottish and very good.

Verity was happy with her new little brother, and her new little brother was happy with everything. Maureen, the kids and Shirley the nanny spent happy times down on the farm in Kent. Meanwhile I spent some time working on a song called 'World' with the wonderful Cat Stevens and his brother David Gordon on another concept album called *Alpha to Omega*. When I first met Cat, or Steve, I instantly liked him and found him to be one of the most charismatic people I have met. We became friends, and although I don't see much of him now I still think of him with affection. And it was a privilege to sing with him on stage at Wembley.

With the new album finished and released in 1979, it was time to think film. I've always had a passion for motorbikes, ever since I borrowed Dad's to bomb down the A13, so I was looking forward very much to the start of filming *Silver Dream Racer*.

It was a great film to make. I was struck by the commitment of the privateer bikers we used in the film. Their love of their bikes surpassed their love of anything, it seemed. They would mortgage their house, wife and family to keep their bikes running. While the top-flight factory-sponsored riders had the weight of Yamaha or Suzuki behind them, these guys just had themselves and a passion for riding. I obviously wanted to do as much of the riding as possible in the film and managed to do quite a lot. I remember the famous bike turning up for the first time. Two special bikes – two Silver Dream machines – were built for the film by a firm called Bartons in Wales, a 500cc and a 750cc. The first one turned up when we were filming at Brands Hatch.

During a break in filming, I got the mechanics to put the bike together and with a push and a cloud of smoke I was off round the track, hitting speeds of over 100mph. The producer was hysterical as he fretted over his star's safety – or so he said. I actually think he was more worried about the Silver Dream machine getting bent.

The power band on a 500cc racing bike is awesome. When it comes in, it's like a punch in the back. The fastest I went on the bike was 140mph on the straight at Silverstone. Nearly as good as playing at Upton Park – West Ham's ground – as I did in a testimonial match a few years ago.

David Wickes, the director, had cast two American actors to play the other lead parts, Cristina Raines and Beau Bridges, who couldn't ride bikes but was a nice fellow. The cast also included my sidekick Clarke Peters, who played Cider. Clark was featured on the soundtrack album and had great success later as a writer and performer with the musical *One Man Named Mo*. It was a happy film to make. Beau was very professional and Cristina interesting and a little neurotic.

With most of the film shot, and the Americans flown off back to Hollywood, David Wickes and I started to talk about the music score I was to write for the film. As this was a new venture for me, we thought it wise to bring in an experienced film orchestrator, and were fortunate to get John Cameron. John was a great help with timings and background music. We would work together many more times, and John is a good friend.

The strained relationship between Maureen and I was taking its toll, and at this point we finally decided to separate in the hope of remaining friends. I based myself at my office in London and set about writing the score for the film. When news of the separation got out, my office was surrounded by journalists and photographers for days. Thankfully, Maureen and the kids were safe and sound in our secret farm in Kent and were not troubled by the media.

I remember Derek going to the door of my office to talk to a journalist from a Sunday tabloid and then hearing him roar with laughter. When he returned, with tears of laughter in his eyes, I asked what was funny. Derek related that this idiot writer had declared that he knew why the separation had happened, which was remarkable as I wasn't even sure of the reason myself. The reason for the break-up, according to the hack, was that I was having a homosexual relationship. I minced around the office and we laughed quite a lot.

Generally over the years the press have been OK to me. There has been the odd kiss-and-tell story, most of them make-believe, but I suppose as I've never gone out of my way to court publicity, I don't seem to have been on their hit-list. It's usual for well publicized people to moan about the intrusion and inaccuracies of the press, but I've found that if you treat them with respect, you're liable to get some back.

The *Silver Dream Racer* score was very interesting to do. I enjoy writing music to accompany visuals and wish I'd done more of it. It's great fun to do those prangs and opening door bits. With the film, of course, there were lots of motor-cycle racing anthems to come up with, as well as the main title song. As I said before, John Cameron helped immensely with the nuts and bolts of timings and incidental music, which left me free to write the main songs and themes. The single, 'Silver Dream Machine', was the hit we hoped for, and the film upon its release in April 1980 was received pretty well. One of my strongest memories of the film was when it was chosen to represent Britain in a film festival in Poland.

Derek and I flew over to Warsaw and were put into a rather depressing hotel in the city centre. After checking in I was shown to a room the size of a broom cupboard. As I suffer with mild claustrophobia it was impossible for me to stay in it, so I asked for another room. The manager replied, 'In Communist Poland everybody has the same.'

'That's fine,' I replied, 'but I can't stay in it so I'll have to leave.' And off I went to get my bags.

'One moment, Mr Essex,' he said, whereupon I was taken to a massive oak-panelled room where apparently the KGB and top politicians stay – a strange form of communism.

It seemed to be a particularly depressing time to be in Warsaw. The rain fell endlessly. There was a food shortage, so from my room I could see lines of poorly dressed people queuing for bread. To top it all, it was Chopin's birthday, so his funeral march seemed always to be on the radio.

There was one bright moment when we went to the showing of the film. The cinema was full of dignitaries, it was quite a to-do. The film started and just before the first line was spoken there was a loud click followed by a deep earth hum, and then it got funny – an interpreter was backstage, mike in hand, speaking a semblance of all the parts in Polish, including the women. David Wickes and I did our best not to cause a diplomatic incident, but by the time the love scenes came on we were in hysterics. I don't think we made too many friends that night in Poland, but for some reason the film did enormously well in South Africa, where it seemed to run for ever.

I've toured South Africa three times and seen many changes over the years. One of our first tours brought a ludicrous ban from a couple of bigoted left-wing councils here in England. Our crime apparently was that on the tour we played a place called Sun City and this was thought somehow to condone apartheid. The fact that half my band were black and the tour played to both black and white people all over South Africa seemed to be irrelevant.

Cape Town is a magical place though. One day Bev and I hired two motorbikes and drove down to the point where the Indian and Atlantic oceans meet. As we rode happily along this wooded cliff face, all of a sudden from out of nowhere five or six mad monkeys hailed down on us. One landed on Bev's head, and I had one on the pillion and one on the handlebars. We were lucky enough to dispatch them before either getting bitten or crashing down into the ocean. It was funny to look back on, but scary at the time.

Funny things, monkeys. I was once in Zimbabwe and walking off the beaten track when a group of monkeys in the trees above became very vocal and agitated, so I decided to turn back. Thank goodness I did, for it turned out that I had been just about to walk into the largest concentration of deadly black mamba snakes in the country. I like to think the monkeys were trying to warn me.

With the publicity around the separation beginning to abate, I started to look for a flat in London for myself – and of course for Verity and Danny when they came to stay. After viewing a few flea-pits I found a flat I liked near Hyde Park. This, I thought, would be good for the kids, as just down the road we had the park to bang about in, plus it was close to my office. So I bought it and moved in.

It was a strange feeling to be single again and quite a change of lifestyle. There were parts of it I enjoyed, but there were many times when I ached to see my children and was consumed by a sense of regret and guilt that I wasn't there with them every day.

Maureen maintained terrific dignity throughout, and we both did our best to present a united and loving friendship to the kids. Many times we took family holidays together and did our utmost to surround the children with our real respect and love for each other. Thankfully this remained the case throughout their childhood. I'm always saddened when breakups occur and the children become casualties. Maureen and I did all we could to give our children the two loving parents they deserved, and even though we were not living together, I think they knew we would never turn our backs on each other and that our mutual love and respect remained very much alive and secure, as it still is today.

# 16

# Hot Love

With *Silver Dream Racer* released and my liaison with John Cameron on the film soundtrack having gone so well, I asked John to work on my next Phonogram album with me. We went into the studio to record *Hot Love* for release later in 1980, coupled with a tour.

The album *Hot Love*, with all the fuss around the film, had the afterburn of motorbikes about it. For one song I'd written called 'On My Bike' I decided to take one of my bikes, a Triumph Bonneville, into the studio and record it as effects in the background of the track. We wheeled the monster through reception and into a vocal booth, the engineer set up some mikes and I kicked it over. Midway through the third take as I revved the engine to the beat, with blue exhaust billowing around me, the world began to spin and it was probably only the quick thinking of the engineer who flung open the door that saved me from a possible mishap. It did sound good, though.

As I was now basically single I was starting to form a few 'hot love' liaisons of my own. The new flat by chance had two entrances and I do remember a sort of French farce when one young lady was being ushered out of one door just as a second lady entered through the other. At least I wasn't caught with my trousers down. I suppose I was in a way making up for lost time and, to be honest, maybe trying to forget the hurt of missing the kids. Don't expect any specifics about relationships from me – I would never go into detail as I have too much respect for the ladies involved. I never have been interested in who is going out with whom, and I think kiss-and-tell stories lack dignity.

I bought Maureen and the kids a house by the Thames in Chiswick and would usually take the kids down to the farm in Kent on Friday nights, or occasionally we would stay in London. I spared them the awkwardness of meeting any of the girlfriends I was seeing, and although of course the set-up was not ideal, we did spend quality time together, maybe even more than if I had been living with them. They suffered my fry-ups and sausage and mash bravely, and I loved spending time with them. Verity was like a little mother to Dan and was a great help. They were very close, the separation probably having brought them closer togeth-er. I hated those Sunday nights when I took them back, and the feeling of emptiness as I drove away was painful. Many times I would stop at the end of the street and think – why?

I decided to buy a family holiday home, where at least the kids could be with Mum and Dad together some of the time. Having spent a fair amount of time in the South of France, I decided on a change and went to look for a place in Spain. I found a farm-house, or *finca* as the locals call it, in the mountains above Marbella. It was a brilliant place complete with its own olive trees, but in need of some work.

Enlisting the help of a local builder, I added a top floor and a swimming pool. The view from the house was fantastic; you could see Gibraltar, and on a clear day you could make out the coast of North Africa. Dotted around in the hills were villas and farm-houses inhabited by local Spanish people on one side of the hill, and a fascinating mix of nationalities on the other – Dutch, Italian, German and English. These foreigners were not on holiday but lived there all the time, and given the remoteness of the location almost certainly had a story – and some of them a history they were trying to avoid.

My nearest neighbour was a larger-than-life Italian named Giovanni. Gio who had a high perimeter fence around his property and a couple of very vicious guard dogs, spent a lot of time drinking and looking over his shoulder. He told me he had flown fighter planes for the Israelis in the Six Day War and, after leaving the air force, had been an Intelligence Officer unearthing Nazi war criminals. Giovanni's stories were impressive. He spent time in Paris as a hell-raiser with the legendary singer and composer Jacques Brel, flew a plane under a bridge in Malaga, much to the annoyance of the local authorities, and generally lived life to the full.

The two of us would meet up and join the nomadic goat herders who roamed the hills. Giovanni, who was a brilliant cook, would rustle up breakfast on an open fire for the shepherds and myself, then act as interpreter between us. The goat guys would slowly cover an area probably a hundred miles wide to graze their herds. With rainfall scarce they were forced into this nomadic lifestyle, using semi-derelict buildings as temporary bases and moving on when the goats had polished off whatever was going.

Giovanni sadly died as the result of an accident. After a drinking session with the shepherds, he fell down a slope and broke his leg very badly. Metal pins were put in to hold it together, and he was supposed to return to hospital to have them taken out, but being the man he was, he didn't bother. The pins rusted and fatally infected his blood stream.

The meetings of the *communidad* were really something and could get very heated, with three or four languages being used at the same time and selective understanding raised to an art. The water well for the community was on our side of the mountain, and the electricity on the Spanish side. With water being a very precious commodity, it seemed from what I could make out that there was much suspicion between the two camps. When the Spanish suspected the foreigners of using too much water they would cut off their electricity, whereupon my lot would turn off their water. It was pretty feudal but thankfully never erupted into shoot-outs, just gentle espionage.

Of course given the shortage of water, my swimming pool was much in debate. To fill it I would get water delivered from town in a tanker, which was fine. The only problem was that when we left, my neighbours would sneak out at dead of night and nick it. In spite of the restless natives, the family and I spent many happy times there.

My son, Danny, and I had one potentially bad experience out in Spain. I used to ride through the mountains on a Honda 250cc off-road bike that I'd brought over from England. Dan loved it. I would sit him in front of me and we'd ride for hours, never seeing another person and kicking up the dust behind us. One day we were riding probably too quickly down a mountain track when, as I got to a bend, I lost the front wheel. Seeing that I was just about to lose it down the side of a cliff, I threw Danny off, and the bike and I then finished up in a heap and a cloud of dust half-way down the mountain.

I have to laugh when I think back, there I was under the bike with a shin bone and knee cap poking out, while Dan stood on top of the mountain angrily shouting, 'What did you do that for?' I think his pride was hurt – I know my leg was.

My children have generally coped well with their daredevil dad, not panicking as I've taken them to the edge too many times. One of them was when I rented a boat in Florida. The only reason the company let me take it was that they knew I was a qualified helicopter pilot and foolishly they thought I knew what I was doing. Sadly boats and I don't really get on. As we headed out to sea, with Verity and Dan safely dressed in life jackets, I went the wrong way round a buoy marker, smashed the propeller on some rocks and had to call out the US Coastguard to rescue us.

Then one time on the Thames I was sick of having to negotiate the locks, so I thought, I wonder if you can go round them – and headed blindly towards a weir. If an astonished fisherman hadn't warned me to turn back, our boat would have gone crashing down a concrete weir, and probably sunk, leaving all of us, including Scruff the dog, to swim to safety.

I was much more conscientious with the flying, but I do remember another sticky moment, again with Dan, when the centrifugal clutch on the main rotor blade failed to engage, forcing me to make an emergency landing in a remote field in Kent. I was worried, and so was the farmer, who thought the SAS had turned up in his cornfield, but I think Dan must have enjoyed the adventure as I never got the telling-off I got with the motorbike incident.

# 17

# Be-Bop-the-Byron

After the mediocre success of the *Hot Love* album and the chasing about with the film and tour, I decided to take up an offer from Cat Stevens, or Yusuf Islam as he has now become, to spend some time in his apartment in Rio. I liked the idea of visiting Brazil, and also wanted to see Argentina and Uruguay, so I packed a bag and went. I was advised to keep a low profile as I don't think *Evita* the musical had gone down too well with the Argentine Junta.

The trip to Argentina was interesting and informative. At the time I was, and still am today, a member of Amnesty International, and the Argentine regime was suspected of causing the disappearance of many of its citizens, the so-called Disappeared Ones – thousands of people who had simply gone missing. I decided to ask some questions.

When I arrived in Buenos Aires the first thing that struck me was how European the city seemed. It even had a Harrods where I bought a pair of socks in the sale. One cannot have enough clean socks when one travels, I find. Not to mention sensible shoes. After settling in I started to meet people and I found the Argentines to be warm and friendly. This was of course before the Falklands.

I met with a young man in a bar who told me in whispers how

his younger sister had been kidnapped and held to ransom. He said she was released after his wealthy father had paid the ransom and that he suspected the military had been responsible for the poor girl's ordeal. Apparently she had been taken in the night, blindfolded and kept tied up in a cave for three weeks. He went on to tell me that she was one of many who had suffered under the shadowy regime that existed in the country at that time. I later met the girl. She was obviously traumatized by what had happened to her and was understandably reluctant to talk about it. I was deeply saddened by the mental scars that were evident to see and suspected her life had been changed for ever. I made some good friends in Buenos Aires and left them with reassurances that I would relate their fate to Amnesty when I returned to England.

Next I caught a plane to Montevideo, the Uruguayan capital. Uruguay I found to be much more Latin American than Argentina, not unlike Cuba. It has a huge number of pristine American Fifties cars, great gas guzzlers that are lovingly maintained by their owners and which sail like galleons through the dusty streets.

One morning, as I was walking by the sea and thinking it was about time I got to Rio, I met two men who were leaning on a rather beaten-up Ford Mustang. I nodded a greeting and they continued a conversation with me in Spanish. Sensing I was from another country, probably because I told them in English that I didn't understand them, one of the chaps, whose name was Jesus, asked me in broken English where I was from. I told him England and he replied, 'Manchester United'. I decided a conversation about West Ham United was a bridge too far, but we got to talking. I told them I was on my way to Rio, and amazingly so were they. They offered me a lift and, not being one to miss out on an adventure, I said thank you.

We arranged to meet in an hour and drive to Brazil. One of

the good things I've found about travelling alone is that you seem to strike up relationships readily and travel paths you would not travel if you were with a companion. Strangers seem more inclined to approach you, probably wondering why you're there and why you're alone. Anyway I grabbed my bag from the guesthouse I was staying in and met the boys down by the beach.

Jesus was a long-haired good-looking man in his thirties, dressed in denim, and with brown eyes that sparkled. He told me he was from Chile and that his friend, who was called Mario, was from Costa Rica. Mario was a rounded guy in a tired-looking blue leisure suit whose only English seemed to be 'Let's boogie' and 'Bobby Charlton'. Putting my bag in the boot, the boys headed for Brazil.

The drive was a long one. I paid my way with the petrol and shared the driving. We would drive long into the night and stop over at very basic hostel-type places to get some sleep, not that I got much as the three of us would share a bed and Mario, if he wasn't snoring, would talk in his sleep in very loud Spanish.

One morning as I took my turn driving we were pulled over by a Brazilian speed cop for going too fast. Jesus and Mario leapt from the car and approached the policeman before he could even get off his bike. A long conversation ensued after which the men shook hands and Jesus and Mario, looking relieved, returned to the car.

'I must drive,' Jesus proclaimed. 'He has let us go but you must never drive again in Brazil.'

'OK,' I replied.

'I told him you English and you used to driving on the wrong side of the road.'

'Thanks,' I replied.

Throughout the trip Mario had been punctuating the miles by rolling these massive spliffs of pure marijuana which were passed around a little too regularly for my liking. Feeling somewhat concerned at the panic they showed when the cop stopped us, I now enquired, 'Where is Mario getting all the combustibles from?'

With a conspiratorial smile Jesus pulled back one of the panels inside the car and, to my horror, showed me the reason why they were on their way to the Rio Carnival – the car was full of drugs. Now I realized why my companions were intent on keeping the speed cop away from the car. As Mario skinned up yet again to his familiar catch-phrase of 'Let's boogie', I sat back and reflected on what the headlines back home might have been as I languished in a cold dark cell somewhere in Brazil.

I was relieved to get to the bright lights of Rio. The boys dropped me off on a street corner and were gone in a smoky blue haze. The vibrancy of Rio was amazing. I'd arrived a week or so before the Carnival was due to begin, and you could feel the excitement in the air. I took a taxi to the apartment to which Yousef had kindly given me keys and for the first time in a while got a good night's sleep. It was good to be the sole occupant of a bed again.

Yusuf's flat was on the side of a hill, spartan but very nice with beautiful views from its balcony. I set off early to explore this magical city. I walked for miles trying to get a feel of the place. It was clearly a city of extremes. Along the Copacabana beach you had multimillion-pound houses and apartments, and just a short distance away there were families living in extreme poverty, housed in tin shacks. I suspected that the Carnival went a long way to keeping the poorer people distracted from the inequality, as they prepared costumes and their Samba Schools most of the year round. It was clear that to be judged the best school was of paramount importance, and it seemed to me that it was probably the pre-occupation of the Carnival and all it stood for that deterred the have-nots from rising up and demanding a more equal society.

This aside, I found the Brazilians to be warm, proud and

friendly. Music seemed to be on every corner. Small bands of percussionists would conjure up wonderful Latin rhythms as red-faced trumpet players blew their hearts out. People danced as they walked. It seemed everybody had an inbuilt sense of rhythm and a joy for living.

One morning I was on one of my walks through Rio when I heard an English voice call 'David?' I turned around and was surprised to see Jim Capaldi, the drummer with Traffic, and the singer of the hit record 'Love Hurts'. Jim told me he was now living in Rio and had married a Brazilian girl. He also had a daughter with whom sadly he could hardly converse as she only spoke Portuguese and he only spoke English, but he was learning fast. He seemed very happy with life and it was good to spend time with him. I remember one night we decided to go for a drink in a hotel and the lift got stuck between the eleventh and twelfth floor. With a lift full of worried people, Jim and I became instant heroes as we forced open the lift doors and pulled the folks to the safety of the twelfth floor.

Another time, while visiting the famous statue of Christ that towers over Rio, I had the good fortune of bumping into Phil Lynott, co-member of the cast of *War of the Worlds* and leading light of the band Thin Lizzy. Phil was on his honeymoon and we struck up a friendship that endured till his sad death a few years later.

Meanwhile back at Yusuf's flat I was starting to get regular visits from persuasive Muslims, I suppose in the hope of converting me to the Muslim faith. I was presented with a copy of the Koran and gently enlightened by two or three friends of Yusuf. I nearly became a convert – but not quite.

The atmosphere in Rio changed dramatically as the Carnival started. It was as though the Devil had taken temporary charge of the place. An atmosphere of decadence prevailed and wave upon wave of colourful Samba Schools cascaded through the crowded streets. Men, women and children, in a manic Samba trance, shuffled and danced mile upon mile. People actually died in the frenzy, it was amazing. Days and nights merged into one as visitors and locals exorcised the frustrations of the year in one massive orgy of music and movement. Now I was no longer in any doubt that the Carnival was a kind of safety valve that blew once a year and kept the people on an even keel for the rest of it.

Having experienced Rio and its Carnival and seen at first hand some of the wonders of South America, it was now time to return to England. All the music I had been surrounded by had started me thinking about my next album. The trip to South America had broadened my horizons, so this time I was looking for something different.

I enjoyed producing myself, but of course it is not always easy to remain objective, so when I returned to England I was looking to take a different path. As luck would have it my old friend Herbie Flowers had been working with American producer Al Kooper. Al and I met and decided to work together, starting in London and finishing in LA.

It was a pleasant change to work with American musicians like guitarists Steve Lukather and Jeff (Skunk) Baxter, and indeed Al Kooper. I think musically the change brought different colours to my songs and I found the change of environment creative. We decided to call the album *Be Bop the Future*, influenced by a new version of Gene Vincent's 'Be Bop a Lulla' that we recorded. Although it received glowing reviews, the album didn't become the big hit we hoped for, but remains one that I'm proud of.

On the way back from recording in LA Derek and I stopped off in my favourite city, New York. While we were there we went to see an Off Broadway production called *Childe Byron* by the American writer Romulus Linney. We both recognized something special in the play, I was so taken with it that I expressed a wish to take the play and present it in London – the American producers agreed.

I had always been interested in Lord Byron, and this highly original play provided a fascinating document of the poet's colourful life. The play begins with Ada, his daughter, in the last hours of her life. Heavily sedated with laudanum, she hallucinates and manifests her father whom, because he was forced by public opinion to leave England, she never got to know. She questions her ghostly father about his life and deeds, which are then illustrated by a larger cast. The play cleverly moves from being a two-hander through scenes of his life which Byron and his daughter watch and react to. This unusual construction makes Linney's work a powerful piece of theatre.

With a commitment from theatre director Frank Dunlop, and having heard that the Young Vic wished to stage the play, I started to research Byron with a passion. He was a remarkable man – mad, bad and dangerous to know seemed to be the consensus. Before rehearsals started, Frank and I decided to take a trip with Sarah Kestelman (who was to play Ada) to the house that Byron inherited as a boy from his Uncle Jack. Mad Jack, as he was known, had apparently shot his best friend in a duel in a darkened room over an argument about the proper mixture of dog food. He would regularly conduct mock battles on the lake in the grounds with the help of terrified servants, who did their best to avoid being hit by cannon balls. He also was famed for lying naked and letting locusts crawl over his body. He died a destitute recluse, and his nephew, young George Gordon, became Lord Byron and inherited the bankrupt estate, Newstead Abbey.

When we got to Newstead it was very impressive. We attempted to gain access, but as luck would have it the house was closed. Refusing to take no for an answer, I was determined after our long drive at least to see inside the house. Stories of ghosts like the Headless Monk and the White Lady had made me curious, so with a leg up from Frank and a 'Be careful' from Sarah I began to shin up a drain pipe. I was making headway when an irate caretaker arrived on the scene and reprimanded me. Climbing back down I explained our mission and the caretaker, Mr Price, kindly let us into the house. It was the start of a love of the place that I have felt ever since. Now run by Nottingham Council, Newstead is still a terrific place to visit. Whenever I'm on tour near Nottingham I always try to get there and see my good friends Maureen and Ken who run the wonderful White Lady restaurant next to the Abbey.

*Childe Byron* ran successfully at the Young Vic from 15 July to 15 August 1981, causing quite a stir. One of my favourite memories of the show was when Richard Burton came to see it and led the audience in a standing ovation. When he came backstage to see me he was very complimentary and said in a broad cockney accent, 'I didn't know you could speak posh, you clever sod.'

# 18

# One-Night Stands in Foreign Lands

I suppose over the years I have been a 'jobbing pop star', by which I mean I have toured and played concerts more than most. In stadiums, theatres and nightclubs all over the world, I've done thousands of one-night stands and I'm proud of the fact that I have never missed a performance. Most of them have been great fun, playing to what I consider to be the best fans on the planet. But some have been a little weird.

A tour was arranged in far away Thailand, consisting of five concerts in Bangkok. My manager Mel had been meeting with a rather shady Far Eastern promoter and had struck a deal. We would receive half our fee before we flew out and the other half on the last night. Mel was a little worried as the promised payment before we left had not materialized, but the band and I wanted to go, and after reassurances from our Far Eastern friend that he would pay us when we arrived, we took a chance, packed our bags and flew to Bangkok.

What a place! It was hot and humid and packed with people who seemed busier than anyone I had ever seen. Coupled with the abundance of Thai sticks that we set fire to probably a few times too often, it began to border on the surreal.

I have a vivid memory of Herbie Flowers and me in the hotel lift, unable to get out of it for what seemed to be hours. There we were, going up and down in a hopeless fashion, laughing uncontrollably as at each stop a new travelling partner filled us with renewed hysterics. I should really have had my suspicions about this tour when one night a box containing dozens of horrible synthetic underpants, mainly beige, was delivered to my door. I was puzzled by this strange present until I saw an ad for the same underpants on TV and gathered that they were sponsoring my tour – Class!

The money had still not turned up, and that night we were supposed to play. I made the decision to do the show anyway, as it was sold out and I felt we shouldn't let people down.

The venue was a very large cinema in the centre of Bangkok. We did our sound-check and did the show in the evening. It went really well and the audience was terrific. It's quite moving to see people who can't speak the language actually managing to sing your lyrics.

Next night we had another good show, but there was still no money and no sign of our local promoter. As the third proposed night came, we had a decision to make. It looked to Mel and me that we had been had. Even so, I decided to finish the shows and maybe work it out later, so off we drove to the cinema. When we got to the venue there were hundreds of confused locals milling around, clearly something was amiss. We made our way through the crowds, only to see a cardboard sign stating in two languages: 'David Essex Show Cancelled – Electrical Problem'. Amazed, we went inside, where to our surprise a film was in progress, with an attentive audience of two. All the sound equipment had been taken away, as the Australian sound company hadn't been paid either. The band and I, with guitars in hand, collapsed in a heap of laughter.

A slightly more productive tour took place in the United Arab Emirates. I actually learned to ice skate in Arabia. The hotel had an ice rink right in the middle of the desert, it was that kind of place.

I remember a strange start to a tour that was kicking off in Ireland. We decided to rent a place near Limerick and rehearse there prior to the first Irish dates.

The house we rented was massive and a little eccentric. It had its own landing strip, some very odd furniture and some mysterious radio transmitting equipment that looked as if it might have belonged to Lord Haw Haw. One night after rehearsals, our driver Michael brought back to the house six bottles of poteen – the Irish firewater made, I believe, from potato. The boys and I gave it a try, and decided it was almost drinkable, so down it went. We were all in a kind of skanky play-room, where there was a snooker table with some balls missing, a dartboard with five plastic darts, and a harp with three strings. Up some steps from the main room was a bar, a radiogram and a couple of dusty standard lamps which lit the room. A strange venue at the best of times, but as the night wore on and the poteen kicked in, it became one of the most bizarre nights I can remember – that's not to say that there are other nights I can't remember.

In one corner you had Mary the housekeeper keeping the peat fire going, in another a band member with a lampshade on his head, while two others played snooker, not with a cue but with their willies. My brilliant sax player, Alan Wakeman, selected a Christmas album by Bing Crosby and proceeded to dance the night away up and down the stairs, not unlike Fred Astaire. I spent a lot of time missing the dartboard and apologizing to Mary for the band's behaviour. 'Oh well,' she replied, 'the boys need to relax.' The best moment was probably when Michael the driver turned up with two girls from the village he had invited to the party – they walked in, saw this bizarre gathering and just walked out again. I think what made it so weird was that everyone seemed in a world of their own. None of the antics were done to impress or make the others laugh; these were things to do and the boys just got busily on with them. Strong stuff, that poteen.

I've also had a few adventures in Australia. I love it there. One time when we played in Perth, I was invited out for an early morning round of golf. I was about to tee off when a nesting emu appeared from the bushes and made a beeline for me. I had to fence it off with my five iron.

Another time, as we drove mile upon mile across Australia, we had an unfortunate collision with a kangaroo. He bounced off and hopped dizzily away while we resigned ourselves to a night's sleep in a seriously broken car.

Touring has been a major part of my life. Maybe it's the gypsy in my soul that enjoys the travel and change, but certainly I find that change is a stimulant and long may it continue.

The travel and the length of my tours, which are much longer than most (I usually do fifty concerts in the UK alone) are really only possible, I think, because of the way the wonderful audiences I have been blessed with help me through. Many times when I have felt weary and jaded the expressions of love and warmth from my concert audiences have made it all worthwhile. In fact I am constantly taken aback by the reaction and am eternally grateful for the strength and energy they have given me for so long. To look down most nights and see three generations of wonderful people relating to my music and myself must be all that a performer could ask for. Thank you.

In 1982 I was approached to front a TV show that to me seemed an interesting project. The BBC wanted to commission a talent show. At first the thought of being a Hughie Green of the Eighties did not appeal to me, but as I thought it through it seemed that with so much talent struggling to reach a wider audience, and so many doors closed, some kind of showcase for new talent would be really worthwhile. So, with a bit of tinkering to the original idea, and after making sure that the acts on the show would be treated with some dignity whether they won or not, I agreed to do it and *The David Essex Showcase* was born.

The show was filmed at the Harrogate Centre in Yorkshire and produced by the late Alan Walsh. Alan would plough through the piles of tapes and videos of hopefuls for the show, and present me with a short list, and together we would decide on the acts that would appear. The show was very popular and gave quite a few acts a chance to demonstrate what they could do – Thomas Dolby, Richard Digance, Mari Wilson, Talk Talk, the Belle Stars and a group who sang the hit 'Coming Home' – a song that coincided with the emotive Falklands War – were all given a start by the *Showcase*.

The band and I would perform a couple of songs from the current self-produced album *Stage Struck* and I would introduce the programme. I enjoyed doing the show and was pleased to try and help some genuine talents receive recognition. There seems to be a real lack of opportunities and openings for new artistes, so hopefully the *Showcase* in its time was of some use.

Around this time there was a brief change in management for me, in the hope of spreading my work in a more international way, especially in a major country I had neglected, the US. By mutual consent from Derek and Mel (who would both still be involved), Elton John's manager John Reid took over.

John liked the *Stage Struck* album and was instrumental in the release of the hit 'Me and My Girl Night Clubbing'. The liaison didn't last long, but I'm glad to say we parted company without any bad feeling at all.

I remember being over at John's house one night when West Ham were playing Watford the next day. I said that the Hammers would win, and John said Elton's Watford would, and that we should take a bet on it. He was prepared to wager his brand new Bentley Mulsanne against my Range Rover. I thought it over and, not being a betting man, plus not having the financial resources that John had, I declined. Lo and behold, West Ham won.

After the decent reaction to the *Stage Struck* album, I again struck up a working relationship with Mike Batt. Together we co-produced the album *The Whisper*, which featured a recurring Christmas hit, 'A Winter's Tale'. Mike and Tim Rice had been working on a lyric for me while I was touring at the end of 1982 and had come up with a song that mirrored the changes in a relationship with the changes in the seasons. As it happened, Mike had just finished work on the film score for *Watership Down* and had considerable success with Art Garfunkel and 'Bright Eyes', so when I came to record my vocal at Air Studios he tried to get me to approach the song in a kind of Art Garfunkel way. Needless to say this didn't happen, but the record certainly did. I think Mike is a massive talent, as a writer, producer and orchestrator. Given the terrific and varied work he has done, he's been dogged too long by the Womble tag (he was the musical force behind the Wombles back in the 1970s) and I think he deserves much more credit than he seems to get. In any case I'd like to know who else could write a string of hits featuring big furry things that pick up litter on Wimbledon Common, I'm not sure I could.

With constant demands on my time and having one of the most recognizable faces in Britain, I decided to renew my acquaintance with my favourite city, New York, and look for a place there to buy. I suppose it was partly because I was looking for a refuge, but also because I found New York to be like an electric source of creativity. With its many live music venues, its theatre and art galleries, it seemed ideal for me: a place full of energy and stimulation where I could move around practically unnoticed.

I therefore set off for New York to look for an apartment. My father had always wanted to visit the Big Apple so I asked him to come with me. Leaving Mum to take care of things at home, Dad had a glint in his eye as he flew out to the new world. He liked New York a lot. We wandered through Little Italy and Chinatown, and even made it to the top of the Empire State Building on a clear day, surveying the island of Manhattan in all its glory.

Being together was brilliant and we had a great time. Dad had reservations about buying a place there; after all I did already have the *finca* in Spain, and he wasn't sure I would even use a New York flat. But I was determined. We visited a downtown real estate office and went on to view a loft at 620 Broadway, close to Greenwich Village.

At first glance it didn't seem very promising. As we stepped over a gaggle of drunks and dead-beats in the entrance of the building, Dad said 'Are you sure?' Maybe I wasn't. We made our way to the lift and went up to see the owner and builder who was selling the lofts.

In this part of town what used to be textile warehouses were now being converted and sold primarily to artists. They tended to be large, open-plan areas and many were used as studios. When the scheme first started you had to obtain an Artist's Certificate to be able to buy one, but now it seemed that they were open to all, and many different kinds of people were buying into the trendy but run-down area.

We entered the sales office and were confronted by a small Jewish man who hurriedly planted a light brown wig on top of his bald head (reminding me of my old employer in the minicab firm). I'm afraid Dad and I got the giggles and most of the sales pitch went in one ear and out the other as we tried without much success to contain ourselves. Sidney, the man with the wonky wig, was very impressed that David Essex was interested in buying a place in his building. 'Having someone like you buying here will attract other buyers,' he said eagerly.

I couldn't see that myself, but he was willing to do all he could to secure the sale. Sid excitedly started showing us the remaining lofts for sale, repeatedly saying that he could transform any space any way I would like. When we got down to the first floor there was a space of about three thousand square feet with enormous windows that overlooked Broadway. Sid was going through all the permutations: 'You could build a wall here, put a balcony there,' and on and on.

We sat down, talked it all through and I went for it. The plan was to split the space into two apartments, so that I could keep one and rent out the other bit to cover the expenses of service charges and things. Sidney assured me that his team of Mexican builders would make the changes in no time, and the deal was done.

Although renting out half of the place seemed like a responsible and sensible thing to do, my passage as a landlord was an education. The first tenant was an Italian dress designer who seemed OK until I started to get complaints from the other residents with regard to his slightly bonkers girlfriend and their tempestuous relationship. I was in England at the time, so I never witnessed the shenanigans at first hand, but it seemed that the madness would start in the early hours of the morning with a loud and violent argument and culminate with the partly clothed, bruised girlfriend sleeping in the lift, waking from time to time to deliver streams of loud Italian curses on various floors. The neighbours were not happy. After much pressure from the Residents' Co-operative I finally got my wayward tenant and his midnight visitor to leave.

The next occupant was a young man called Sol who maintained he invented those tags on clothing that are supposed to prevent shoplifting. Sol was a friendly and likeable soul and things went well at first, although I was a little worried one time when he invited me into his flat. While I was there the entryphone went, and three massive guys walked in with a cocaine rock the size of a small football ready to do business. Fair enough, but one was wearing stockings and high heels. I wondered why my neighbour seemed to have trouble sleeping. Sol finally had the whistle blown on him when he decided to purchase a wolf as a pet. The Co-op rose up again and Sol was gone in a cloud of white powder.

The final straw for my friends in the Co-op came from what I, in good faith, thought was a good turn. The janitor for the building was a black man called James who lived with his wife in a tiny space in the basement next to the heating system. Feeling sorry for them, and given the fact that I was hardly there, I handed James my keys and said he and Mrs James could use my place when I wasn't there – really to release them from the dungeon they were living in.

James had keys to most apartments, so I was confident all would be well. No prizes for guessing that it wasn't. One morning my phone rang in London and it was the New York police. It seemed, using my loft as a base, James had emptied the unoccupied lofts in the building and stored the stuff in my place. Then a couple of his relatives had driven up from Louisiana in a truck, loaded the goods on to it, including all of my stuff, except for a sofa that remained on the sidewalk below, and they had disappeared into the night. Also my loft was littered with syringes from drug use and there was blood from injections spattered over some of the walls. Needless to say the Co-op was so hysterical that shortly afterwards I decided to sell up. I sold the loft to a very conservative Chinese Wall Street financial adviser – and at a profit.

I had some wonderful times living in New York. I was invited to Andy Warhol's house, met up with John Lennon, and my friend Chris Spedding the guitarist lived around the corner. I even met Carlotta my future wife there.

One night in 1984 I was at a loose end and looked at the *Village Voice* newspaper to see what was going on. That night at CBGBs, a venue often referred to as the birthplace of punk, there was a band called 'A Rash of Stabbings'.

That sounds interesting, I thought, so I decided to walk around the corner to the Bowery and take a look. When I got to the club, 'Rash' were in the middle of a thundering set and amid the commotion was this small pretty girl, with one side of her hair shaved and the other side over one eye. Her stage presence was special, as she attacked the mikes, and a guitar that looked a size too big for her, with equal ferocity. I was really struck by her and arranged to meet the band afterwards. What I had in mind at the time was to explore the possibility of maybe producing the band. We met and, although the producing thing never took place, it was the start of a transatlantic love affair that led to Carlotta leaving the band, coming to visit me in London and eventually moving to England.

# 19

# Flying Down to Fairoaks

Ever since I was a little boy and used to watch the American TV programme *Whirlybirds* I have been fascinated by helicopters, but it was after a conversation with my friend Kenney Jones that I decided to take lessons and attempt to get one airborne. Kenney was about to embark on a training course at Fairoaks Airport in the hope of becoming a qualified private helicopter pilot. Memories of Buzz (one of the heroes of the *Whirlybirds*) came to mind, and I decided to join him.

The training of pilots is a serious business. Unlike fixed-wing aircraft, helicopters seem to defy the basic logic of aerodynamics by simply staying in the air. They are also more difficult to fly than aeroplanes, so in the various armed services helicopter pilots are looked upon as a slightly unusual breed. I remember an ex-Navy pilot saying to me that as long as you fly a helicopter as if you're waiting for a disaster to happen, you won't go far wrong. He also recommended that to be an inherent coward was essential as well. By this I took him to mean that while you're flying you should be scared and aware of everything. Not bad advice, but a little harrowing.

With some trepidation I reported for my first lesson under my instructor Captain Ken Summers. An ex-Army pilot, originally from Nottingham, Ken was a fit man with penetrating brown eyes, straightforward and, unlike his job, very down to earth.

Kenney and I decided to get our rating on the Bell 47 heli-copter. That's the one you see in the titles of the American TV comedy *M\*A\*S\*H*. Essentially it's a plastic bubble with some scaf-folding on the back, a fairly basic and in some ways rather diffi-cult helicopter to fly, as it doesn't have some of the labour-saving devices that the more sophisticated choppers have.

Captain Summers was a good instructor, he was patient and encouraging and apart from what seemed to be his stock phrase when I made a heavier than perfect landing – 'You bounced it' – he led Kenney and me very successfully through our training. It seemed that we were both able to master the physical aspects of flying the thing quicker than most, probably because as drummers we were used to doing different things with both our hands and our feet. When flying helicopters, this is very useful, for at any given time you seem to be doing five things at once. The written exams were quite a stretch, but with the aid of a bucketful of reading and revision I managed to pass them.

I'll never forget my first solo flight. Over the weeks I had flown about nine or ten hours under instruction, with Cap'n Ken by my side, gently taking me through my paces. On this landmark morning, Ken and I had flown a few circuits and gone through an emergency landing, when to my surprise Ken told me to land. I made a good job of the approach into wind, but landed a little heavily from the hover. Ken of course gave me the 'You bounced it' line, unstrapped himself, got out, looked at the sky, threw a piece of grass in the air to determine the wind direction, came back to the cockpit, radioed the control tower to let them know, and said, 'Right, David, you're on your own. Remember all I've taught you.' Then he shook my hand and walked away.

Thinking back, it must have been a decision of some gravity for Ken. If his confidence was misplaced and a pupil was allowed to fly solo too early, the results could be disastrous.

This was big. The airfield suddenly seemed surreal as my mind raced and a heady mixture of excitement and nervousness filled the cockpit. I radioed the control tower for permission to take off – and took off. The helicopter was up and away and I was all alone. The phrase 'scary but good' came to mind. It was amazing, and I even landed without 'bouncing it', to be congratulated by Captain Ken, the control tower and all the rest of the pilots. It was a day to remember.

As was my first solo cross country a few weeks later. As part of the final exams I had to fly to a designated airfield, land, refuel and get a paper signed by the control tower to say I'd made it. Goodwood Airfield was selected as my port of call. I meticulously planned my flight, plotting wind direction and compass headings, and made Goodwood without any problems. Feeling pretty relaxed and with my paper signed, I took off for the flight back to Fairoaks, carefully watching my headings and following the map. I must have been thirty or so miles from base when Farnborough came up with a call for me to change my heading immediately. Slightly panicked, as I was now heading towards Wales, I was just about to ask why when three jet fighters went screaming by. Farnborough came back with 'Helicopter Golf Whisky Juliet India Lema – You may proceed on your previous heading.'

Thanks, I thought, as I radioed 'Willco.' But where was I? Thank goodness for the M25! I was able to follow it round and finally get back to base, successfully completing my first solo cross country – with no thanks to the Royal Air Force.

After Kenney and I passed and became qualified we came across a Bell 47 that belonged to the Army and had spent most of its life in a crate in Egypt. We decided to buy it together and share the flying hours between us.

In years to come I flew on a couple of my rock tours, landing at hotels or local airfields. I'd also make frequent flights over to Mum and Dad's house, until Mum banned me from landing in the garden because I blew most of the flowers off her rhododendrons. It was great to take Dad on a low-level flight over the docks where he used to work. He was very proud as he pointed out the different areas that had shaped so much of his life. I also remember taking Mum on a sunset flight over the hopfields of Kent. She loved it.

All in all it was, I feel, an achievement to become 'Captain Cook', and I enjoyed the challenge very much.

# 20

# Captain Cook and the South Seas

At the end of 1983 I began thinking that as I had appeared in other people's musicals and was a writer of songs it would seem logical to put the two together and write my own musical. I have always found the leap from spoken word to breaking out in song in some musicals a little awkward, so I started to look for a subject that I felt could carry music in a credible way.

I first started to think about some of the dark and fascinating Grimm's Fairy Tales that have strangeness and magic interwoven in their fabric. It was Derek who suggested the mutiny that happened on HMS *Bounty*. At first I wasn't sold on the idea but as I looked into it, it seemed more and more to be a subject big enough to hold music. After all, a fiddler was used on ship as the sailors were encouraged to dance to maintain fitness – the first form of aerobics, I suppose. The storm sequences certainly cried out for expansive music, and of course you had the relief of the textures and colours of Polynesian music when the *Bounty* landed in Tahiti. That, coupled with the conflict of ideals between Fletcher Christian and William Bligh seemed to me to make the mutiny that happened in the South Seas the right subject-matter.

Derek had heard of a playwright called Richard Crane, who had already written a children's version of *Mutiny on the Bounty* which later I'd read with interest, so a meeting was set up between us. I was unsure how the process of collaborating would sit with me, never having done it, but for something as ambitious as this, I realized that probably two heads would be better than one.

I travelled down to Brighton, where Richard lived. I think we got on well immediately. Richard was about my age and had a boyish charm and a deep-felt passion for and knowledge of the subject. We decided we could and would work together.

Over the long process of writing *Mutiny*, Richard concentrated on the book and I concentrated on the music and lyrics. *Mutiny*, moved through many changes and re-writes on its eventual journey to the West End.

The first theatre director in line for staging the show was the Royal Shakespeare Company's Terry Hands. Terry wanted the Ballet Rambert's choreographer and leading dance light Christopher Bruce to stage the dance sequences. Christopher agreed, and although the show was not yet totally finished, it was reassuring to have these two major talents involved.

The assembled creative team went about their own research into the subject, reading up and delving into all aspects of the famous mutiny. We decided a trip to Tahiti was essential – honest, you know, to see the island at first hand and hopefully meet some of the descendants of the original mutineers who still lived in the South Seas. I was hoping to get to Pitcairn Island, where Fletcher Christian went to hide and where he finished his days. So eventually a trip was planned for Terry, Christopher and me to go to the far-off island of Tahiti.

The flight was long but we were filled with anticipation, anxious to see for ourselves why this island was pivotal to the mutiny. We finally landed at about one in the morning Tahiti time and, like the crew of the *Bounty* many years earlier, as I set foot on the island, I was enchanted.

In the warm night sky a big yellow moon shone down from the star-filled back drop, perfumed flowers filled the air with their exotic fragrance. Yes, it did feel like paradise and you could understand how wonderful the place must have seemed after months and months of battling storms, cramped quarters, severe discipline and poor diet. Here was a place where fresh food was abundant, the natives were friendly and the sun always shone. Paradise indeed for those embattled sailors of the King's Navy in the seventeen-eighties.

We were met at the airport with the traditional greeting of flowers draped around our necks and then driven to our hotel, a beautiful location where log bungalow-type accommodation sat in the incredibly blue Pacific Ocean. From my balcony I could see the island of Moorea in the distance, it was a truly breathtaking place.

We three modern-day mutineers spent a wonderful and informative two weeks there. Chris studied the local traditional dances, Terry met with descendants of the actual mutineers, and I listened to and started to write music. The hit 'Tahiti' was written on my balcony with the help of a hired keyboard and a stunning sunset.

It was not all work, and I use that term lightly, as we did venture into the rather bizarre night-life of the place. Papeete, the capital of Tahiti, is also a major port and base for the French Navy who have, as the mutineers had before them, a great appetite for all that shore leave entails. The difference is that since the mutineers' day, when stories of the openness of the women of the South Seas were legendary, the Catholic Church has made serious in-roads and attitudes to sex have tightened considerably.

One night we went into a place called the Piano Bar. I was at first taken with what seemed to be several beautiful girls but soon realized that every she was a he. I suppose the lady-boys were filling a void left by the rather chaste women.

After an hour or so as we sat and watched from the safety of a corner table, the 'girls' began sensing that we were certainly not after the same thing as some of the drunken sailors, and four lady-boys befriended us and came to sit with us. Then, out of nowhere, a jealous and very drunk sailor who apparently had been dancing with one of the 'girls' decided to attack us with a bottle. As he lurched toward us one of the 'girls' stood up in a leopardskin miniskirt and hit him with a right hook worthy of Mike Tyson in his prime. It was amazing – he crashed over the table and was thrown head first out into the street by what looked like some beautiful but deadly 'girls'. We thanked them but decided not to visit again.

I tried very hard to get to the remote Pitcairn Island, where Christian and the mutineers found refuge from the British Navy after 1789, but was informed I would have to take pot luck and wait for a ship that was passing Pitcairn to deliver post and supplies, which could mean waiting six months or so. It would have been good to talk to the direct descendants of Christian, Adams and the others, but not this time. Adams was actually given a Royal Pardon in later years for becoming a devout Christian and leading the islanders to Christianity, while sadly the other mutineers either killed themselves or each other. Fletcher Christian became a recluse and finally committed suicide by throwing himself from a cliff. It would have been fascinating to talk to their grandchildren, but it was not to be. Still, thanks to our experiences of the South Seas we flew home with a clearer picture of Tahiti and the spell it could cast.

On our return the writing and preparations for the opening started to gain momentum. I finished the score and John Cameron and I prepared to record a concept album of the show, with the aim of building up interest in the show in advance.

My first choice for the part of Captain Bligh was the wonderful Frank Finlay and I was thrilled when Frank agreed to do it. I was equally thrilled when, after meeting the leader of the Royal Philharmonic Orchestra and playing him my score, he congratulated me and agreed that the orchestra would record with me.

The recording of the *Mutiny* concept album was both nerve-racking and tremendously exciting. To hear the Royal Philharmonic play my music and see it start to come alive as the terrific cast I was able to enlist breathed life into their respective characters was a fantastic experience.

We released the album in 1983, and the top-ten hit 'Tahiti' helped to blaze the way for an eventual much publicized opening.

Now although the project was steering a positive course, a venue for the epic was proving hard to come by. At one time we were ready to go into the Theatre Royal Drury Lane but lost it to *42nd Street*, so time scales were getting out of whack. Terry Hands had committed a certain time to stage the show but as time dragged on had to leave in order to honour his commitments to the Royal Shakespeare Company. More time went by until, now without a director or a theatre to house it, the *Bounty* was in danger of sinking without trace.

The producers Howard Panter and Bill Freedman did their best to secure investors in the show and to find a theatre for its home, but my biggest concern was to replace the director.

Derek suggested we should go and see a show that was playing at the National Theatre based on *The Rhyme of the Ancient Mariner*, directed by Michael Bogdanov. We went, and liked what we saw. There were boats and sailors, which seemed pretty relevant, so we approached Michael and although he had some opera productions to direct in Germany he was very enthusiastic about becoming involved.

With Michael on board the character of the piece slowly started to change. William Dudley had been commissioned to design the set and under Terry Hands' direction had developed a kind of abstract set using sails and space. Michael wanted a boat.

William went away and came up with an incredible replica of HMS *Bounty*. It was almost actual size and traversed and pitched on a complicated hydraulic system that would be housed deep in

*Above:* Frank Finlay and me charting a course through the critic-infested waters of the West End. *Right:* Playing the mad, bad and dangerous to know Lord Byron at the Young Vic. *Below:* Shooting a video in the California Desert for Billy Swan: me, Billy, Kenney Jones and Roger McGuinn.

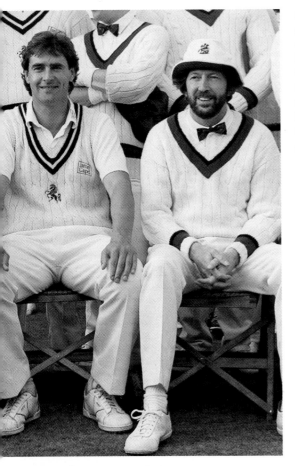

*Far Left:* Looking rather lovely on a surf board shooting a video for the single *Look At The Sun Shining. Left*: Turning out for the now defunct Eric Clapton XI. Left to right: cricket legend Colin Cowdrey, me, his son Chris and Eric Clapton. *Bottom right*: Cricket is like a religion in the Caribbean. Here I am pictured on a trip for VSO to the islands. *Bottom left:* Captain Cook in his plastic bubble with a bit of scaffolding at the back.

*Opposite page, top:* In Malawi, making good use of
the footballs West Ham United donated for one of
my trips to Africa. *Below:* The wonderful cast of
*Godspell* in Uganda react to a piece of magic.

*Right:* The cast prepare for an opening at the
National Theatre in Uganda. *Below:* Saying hello
backstage after a Royal Variety Show.

*Left:* Filming the BBC series *The River* in the idyllic, but slightly smelly, Chumley-on-Water, 1988. *Below:* My twin sons Bill and Kit, born on 19th May 1988, just after leaving intensive care weighing just over 3lbs each and two months premature.

*Opposite top:* Me, George, Bill and Kit in the garden. George is the furry one. *Below:* I was so proud when my boys ran out at Upton Park. Here they are pictured with the Under 11 West Ham squad: both in the front row, Kit third from left, Bill second from right. I wish all the boys well.

Verity, Mum and Dan at Buckingham Palace to witness my investiture.

My daughter Verity's wedding – a magical day, December 9th 2001.

the bowels of the stage. The rigging and sails were to be flown in the flies above the stage and the cast would literally build the boat in front of the audience. All in all it was a fantastic set, as anyone who saw the show would agree. Meanwhile the search for a theatre was moving forward. Because of the depth needed to house the hydraulics and the stage size needed to fit the boat, options were limited.

The producers came up with the Piccadilly Theatre. I must say that I had real reservations, as the Piccadilly is tucked away in a backwater behind Piccadilly Circus and has a history of shows closing through lack of business. But left with few options and desperate to get the thing on, we finally settled on the Piccadilly Theatre.

Through 1983 and 1984, as we tinkered and waited for the theatre, *Mutiny* was taking up most of my time, but I was still recording and touring with albums like *This One's For You* and singles such as 'Falling Angels Riding' and 'Welcome' (both tunes were later included in the *Mutiny* score).

I flew a couple of British tours in my new mode of transport, the helicopter. It was a challenge working out landing sites for the many venues. My security man at the time and for a few years before was the wonderful John Ferguson. John was a former parachute regiment soldier, and I'm sure that as he accompanied me on the flights there were times when he wished he'd packed a parachute!

There was one trip from Bournemouth to Northampton when we hit an electrical storm in Bath. I descended to about five hundred feet, and we flew around Bath for a while until an opening in the storm came and then proceeded bumpily on our way.

At the beginning of 1985, with the Piccadilly Theatre set we finally started to cast the show. Having Christopher Bruce as our choreographer meant we were assured of terrific dancers and we got them. We also held what are called open auditions, which as the name suggests means they are open to all and sundry. These auditions are a little like a cattle market, and although we tried to conduct them with as much dignity as possible, the level of talent always varies greatly from good to 'why?'

I remember one long day when the standard of would-be stars was particularly indifferent and I was starting to lose it in a fit of giggles. The final straw came for me when this particular hopeful bounced on stage and sang a medley of some very out-of-tune songs from that dodgy score *Chitty Chitty Bang Bang* while at the same time attempting to do fire-eating in the instrumental breaks. That was it. I crawled as silently as possible under my seat to take refuge in a broom cupboard at the back of the auditorium, only to find it already occupied by a giggling producer.

We did finally assemble a brilliant cast, headed by Frank Finlay who was an example to us all, and rehearsals started in late May of 1985 at a hall in Wandsworth, London.

The rehearsals were very physical. After all, we had rigging to climb, hornpipes to dance and storms to overcome, but it was a very happy and enthusiastic company. Frank was wonderful and threw himself into proceedings like a twenty-year-old but opted out of the five-a-side football matches in the lunch break. Day by day I watched as Richard's words took on life and my music began to breathe as the characters slowly began to make it their own. A dream was becoming a reality. Little did we know at this stage what a nightmare the technical rehearsals would be.

While we polished the musical in rehearsal, a team of construction workers were digging down deep below the Piccadilly Theatre stage, so deep in fact that they were in danger of hitting the Piccadilly Line below them. The complicated hydraulic system needed to house and work the ship meant excavating some hundred feet. I'm told that the site was used as a burial ground at the time of the plague, but luckily no skeletons were found.

With the hydraulics and ship finally installed, rehearsals moved from the hall in Wandsworth and into the theatre itself. Without any doubt it was the most complicated and dangerous set you could wish to work on. Quite simply, as the boat pitched and tossed as it rounded the imaginary Cape Horn, if you fell from the rigging you were dead.

This of course did not help the singing and acting, as most of our energies at the beginning were focused on simply staying alive. The patience of the cast and the stage crew during the technical rehearsals was saint-like. Michael spent endless hours attempting to get the monster ship to behave, aided by a bottle of Jamesons Irish whiskey. Mickey, the lady who operated the ship, had a really difficult time as frequently it seemed to have a mind of its own and would crash into the back wall of the theatre, with broken stage lights cascading over the long-suffering actors below. Thankfully we all remained intact, but owing to the technical difficulties the planned date for our opening had to be put back twice.

The public previews were cut to a minimum, so at the time of the first night there was still an air of insecurity about the ship and its behaviour. In truth I suspect we were not really ready to open, but under pressure from the producers to get the thing on, the show opened the day after my 38th birthday on 24 July 1985.

The opening night went very well and was greeted by an enthusiastic standing ovation from the audience, but more importantly we all lived through it.

One lasting friendship was formed when Mel organized a security man to get me in and out of the theatre. He was called Mick or Mick the Greek. Mick is now like a brother to me and has worked with me ever since. We have travelled many miles together and shared many experiences.

The first-night party was full of relief, excitement and the media. Everybody seemed to love the show. Many people said it was the best musical they had ever seen, so it came as a complete surprise when I read the reviews the next morning. It seemed to Derek and me that as far as the critics were concerned I had stepped above my station. We were aware that the only other people to write a musical and star in it were Noël Coward and Anthony Newley. Fair enough, but I think I know what works and what doesn't and *Mutiny*, although it may have opened before it was totally secure, did work. The standing ovations night after night proved that, and although most of the critics did their best to scupper the show, and some crisis was reducing the number of foreign tourists coming to London during a period of the run, *Mutiny* sailed on for almost a year and a half.

For me personally it was special to see a dream materialize, and although it was difficult to carry so much of the weight of the thing on my shoulders, the cast and producers were always supportive and the audience reaction was always uplifting. Even the ship behaved most of the time, only caressing the back wall occasionally. One time I remember the ship did play up, and overshot its mark during a scene which involved a burial at sea, leaving the cast facing upstage with the audience behind us. Dear Frank, who is a little short-sighted, was either unaware of this or supremely professional, and played his rather important speech to an attentive back wall. We were all trying to remain as sombre as possible as the occasion demanded, until my dear friend Bill Snape, who played a fat cook, slipped on the misplaced steps below deck and blew off in the process, triggering a giggling fit from the Union Jack-draped dead body which quickly spread through the funeral while Frank carried on regardless.

The run of *Mutiny* was plagued for me with colds and fatigue. Whether it was the strain of trying to make your own show a success, or whether perhaps the builders had disturbed the remnants of the plague with their excavations, I don't know, but I managed to perform every show, keeping my unblemished record of never missing a show or concert throughout my entire career.

I remember one matinee feeling really rough, and as luck would have it that was the day Cliff Richard and the cast of a musical he was then doing called *Time* came to see what all the fuss was about, only to hear me growl through my songs like Lee Marvin.

By the end of the run I had had enough and was grateful when the final curtain came down one Saturday in November 1986. By the following Monday I was on a plane bound for India and away from it all.

# 21

# Green in a Pink City

After the battle to keep the show afloat and a seemingly constant tabloid interest in my private life, a trip to India, such a contrast with the confines of eight shows a week in the same theatre, seemed a good idea. I was interested in the spirituality of India, and partial to a curry, so off I went. Carrying very few possessions but with my credit card for a safety net, I landed in Delhi. I intended to see as much of this very big country as possible and in as much of a grassroots way as I could.

If you haven't been to India let me tell you it is a truly remarkable place. It seems every conceivable mode of transport clogs the bumpy roads, punctuated by wandering cows. The poverty in some places is heartbreaking, especially as it sits side by side with bejewelled temples.

Everything is crowded, there are people everywhere, and in places like Bombay and Delhi a distinct smell of spice laced with sewage floats on the humid air. But there is little doubt that there is a spirituality about the country.

Given my own personal heritage, from a gypsy background, I could see in Indian dress and appearance a link with what we think of as classic gypsy looks. After all, this is where the world's travelling populations were supposed to have started from, and in the women of Goa I could see those Romany roots.

I also noticed that some serious job creation goes on in India. One day I decided to go and see a museum in Bombay. I lined up for a ticket, and was given a ticket to go and get a ticket. I got the ticket and was sent to another bloke who looked at my ticket and then sent me to another chap who stamped my ticket and sent me to another bloke who tore off a bit of my stamped ticket and sent me to another line where they carefully logged the number of my ticket. The guy there sent me to another bloke who took my ticket, and in I went – as easy as that.

I don't know if I was unlucky, but full of expectations I wandered into a few friendly eating establishments to sample a curry in the place of its birth. It wasn't good. What we have in our local high street is quite different from the stuff I was given, which was like bones in spicy gravy, but at least the chapati was good.

As I travelled, I tried to stay in bed and breakfast places owned by local people. Knowing that big hotels are pretty much the same the world over, and having spent much of my life in them, I had little interest in using them. That reminds me of the American singer Lou Reed telling me he had decorated his New York apartment like a Holiday Inn room so that when he was on tour he felt like he was at home.

In Bombay I was befriended by two Air India air hostesses, one of whom let me stay in her house. Her boyfriend had a motorbike and kindly let me use it. Negotiating the mayhem of Bombay traffic was a challenge – I think the cows won.

One day I rode past a very unusual place where vultures circled overhead. There was a massive wall where I saw men with beards down to their waists and fingernails to match. I related what I'd seen to my hosts that evening and asked what the myste-rious place was. I was told that these men belonged to one of the many religions that abound in India. They don't cut their hair or nails, and when they die their bodies are stood up in what is called the Towers of Silence whereupon the vultures eat them. Definitely not a place to sunbathe.

As I set off on the train from Bombay to Agra to see the Taj Mahal the sun was just rising. It looked beautiful breaking through the morning mist as we pulled out from the station. The spell was soon well and truly broken, however, as all along the track side the locals were going about their daily ablutions, which included some rather generous bowel movements. The train was packed but soon we arrived in Agra.

By the time we arrived clouds had covered the sky, which in a way gave the dazzling white Taj Mahal an even more majestic and dramatic aura. Built for his wife by the Emperor Shah Jahan, this wonderful gift of love framed by the dark grey sky was truly impressive.

Next I set off for the famous 'pink city' of Jaipur. As I had been sleeping in some fairly rough places I decided to check into a hotel I'd seen in an advertisement that looked pretty smart. When I got to Jaipur, which is indeed mostly pink, I boarded a sort of scooter taxi thing and we headed to the hotel. Thoughts of a bath, a comfortable bed and decent food started to come into my mind. Soon we were bouncing up the drive to a very grand-looking hotel. I paid my friendly scooter man some rupees and went to check in, only to be told they were closed for refurbishment. Coming back outside I found my scooter man still there so I asked him if he knew of a nice place to stay for a couple of days. He told me of a maharaja who was a little down on his luck but who lived in a palace and, if he liked the look of a prospective guest, would rent you a room.

'Let's go.'

As we travelled the streets of Jaipur the conversation turned to cricket, and this bloke knew his stuff. It's sad that cricket in England seems to have become an elitist secondary sport. What a contrast with the subcontinent and the Caribbean, where the sport is almost a religion.

We turned a corner and into the driveway of an enormous house. My cricket friend waited as I went looking for signs of life. Before I had a chance to find the bell, the massive front door opened and there stood a turbaned servant. Thankfully he spoke perfect English and was very helpful. I explained I needed a room for two or three nights, and he went off to talk to the maharaja.

My wish was granted and I didn't even have to rub a lamp. I gave my friend a wave and some more rupees and went inside. It was an amazing place, tigers' heads adorned the walls, elephant tusks – the lot. It was the old Raj, but very much in decline. The gold in the palace had lost some of its glitter and the peacocks that strutted the unkempt grounds were a little fleabitten but, hey, it was home.

My bedroom was enormous, red and gold with a four-poster bed that was as hard as a rock, and an abundance of stuffed hunting trophies. Including of course a stuffed tiger head – no wonder there ain't many left. Dinner was just an hour away, I was informed, so I had a welcome bath and changed for dinner.

A gong sounded – the universal language for 'Grub's up' – and I wandered out into the hall. I was soon ushered into the dining hall, which was grand and very large. In the middle was a table big enough to seat at least twenty people, with just one place set and ten waiters. I was shown to the seat and sat self-consciously down.

It was pretty strange being waited on by a small army. At the slightest movement from me, three servants would leap to my aid. Now and again two beautiful little girls would poke their heads around a corner and giggle at me. The food was pretty good, but the over-attentive service made me feel awkward, it felt like every move I made was being witnessed in a much too servile way.

After finally getting used to the hardest bed in the world, I slept well and after more over-attentive service at breakfast decided to head off and see some Hindu temples. They were wonderful, and I even rode an elephant, so it was a good day.

After trekking for miles in the hot sun I saw a man selling ice cream. Just the job, I thought, and assumed that if there were any dodgy germs they would be frozen and killed. But they don't die, do they. I knew I should have listened to Daddy Dines in the science lessons, they just lie dormant till they thaw out. I don't think I have ever been so sick in my life. I'm sorry but we're not talking ordinary sick here – it was as if a hosepipe was connected to my mouth. By the time I got back to the maharaja's place I was feeling weak. My waiters seemed concerned, probably because any waiting tonight was right out of the question. I headed straight to bed.

By the early morning I was delirious and dehydrated and of course in very weird surroundings – the tiger on the wall was starting to move in for the kill. Then the maharaja came into my room, followed by a local doctor. Although I could see them, it felt as if they were in another world. All of a sudden Doc presented this gigantic hypodermic needle, stuck it into my arm and told me to take some brightly coloured tablets at regular intervals. Then they were gone, and so was I for about eight hours.

I wonder sometimes, if that quiet maharaja with the giggling daughters hadn't been so concerned and kind, how ill I might have become. Anyway, after a couple of days I was back on my feet and ready to move on. I thanked my host and with one last giggle from the girls made my way to the slightly different world of Goa.

Goa as you probably know has a large Portuguese influence and a reputation for housing hippies. Apart from nearly drowning on an overcrowded ferry that gave up the ghost and sank, my visit to Goa was very enjoyable. It seemed strange to see all that Portuguese architecture in India, and likewise the sandal-clad hippies who seem to litter the coast. Time to go north, I thought.

I caught a plane to Srinigar in Kashmir at the foot of the Himalayas. Here the air felt fresh and clean. Kashmir was beautiful, with its great lakes dotted with curious Victorian-style houseboats. It seems that the British colonials were not allowed to buy land there, so they built these strange houseboats on the lakes.

I managed to rent one and it was brilliant. People would float by, selling everything you wanted. I even got measured for a shirt, and the shirtmaker made it and brought it back the same day.

The tranquillity of the place was occasionally interrupted by the sound of distant gun-fire from the disputed Kashmir border between India and Pakistan, but it was a wonderfully restful place to spend a few days. Looking back on my Indian adventure I had a very interesting trip and probably enjoyed the stay in Kashmir most of all.

It was half-way up a mountain in Kashmir that I was fortunate to meet with a holy man dressed in sun-faded orange robes. We sat and spoke for hours. These holy men wander India and are fed and sheltered by households they choose to visit. To receive them is thought by most to be a great honour. He talked of the many passages of life and death and the lessons we must learn in our many reincarnations. He said he recognized in me a kindred and much travelled spirit and wondered if I was in fact a holy man in my own land. I told him I was a musician.

# 22

# Touching the Ghost

I left India in time to get back to England for Christmas. I had missed Verity and Danny a lot, so it was wonderful to see them and relate my stories and listen to theirs. We had a lovely Christmas and it felt good to be free of the *Mutiny* show. As 1987 dawned I was starting to think about touring and recording again. Having spent nearly two years focused on theatre, I was looking forward to returning to music and feeling that the break would make touring and recording a nice change.

It was around this time that I was approached to make a guest appearance on an album put together by Mike Read. Mike had written music to poems by the late Poet Laureate Sir John Betjeman. I agreed and recorded a musical version of Sir John's lovely poem 'Myfanwy', which did very well. Now I was looking to record my own songs.

In the spring I started writing the *Touching the Ghost* album. The title track was not about ghosts as such, although as I told you I'm sure I've seen one, but about the strange, intangible process of song writing, which is almost impossible to explain. I've known many virtuoso musicians over the years who, although excellent musicians, are unable to compose a catchy melody and lyric that relates to a wide audience, which I suppose makes the ability to write hit songs even more mysterious.

When I sit down to write it is usually under some pressure. Either the studio has been booked or I'm behind the recording company's schedule. I think I put it off because although it's rewarding for me, it's a little painful. Though, over the years, I have composed something like two days and nights' worth of music.

Usually I sit at the keyboards and certain chords start to suggest pictures of lyrics and melodies. Working out where these initial sparks come from is like trying to touch a ghost, hence the title. Once I have found an idea I'm happy with, then it becomes more of a straightforward process. I suppose you draw upon your experience to develop the initial and mysterious spark into a finished song.

It is very special when songs you have written become part of the social fabric, or a letter arrives saying how a particular song you have written means so much to somebody. I am truly grateful that I seem to have been blessed with the gift of song writing. I suspect that if I had been a singer of other people's songs I would have felt a little shallow and would not in the long term have been able to show the kind of commitment to other writers' ideas that I can to my own. At least I know what I'm singing about.

With most of the songs written for the *Touching the Ghost* album, I started to think about a producer. I didn't want to do it myself and in the back of my mind I thought maybe Jeff Wayne and I had some unfinished creative business, so I gave Jeff a ring.

I wasn't sure how he would react. I suppose both our egos had been a little bruised by the parting of the ways, but we had remained friends, as I'm pleased to say we still are today. Jeff's reaction on the phone was positive, so I drove over to his studio in Hertfordshire to play him what I'd written.

Tentatively I knocked on the big door of Jeff's big house. The door opened and there was Jeff with a big hug for his old mate and a box of plasters and bandages he had ordered for the sessions, just in case.

It was surprising how easily we picked up where we had left off. Soon ideas were buzzing. We decided just to work on a couple of tracks, to test the water. The remainder would be co-produced by me and Ian Wherry, my impressive keyboard player and a producer in his own right. But the writing and recording would take another two years before the album was finally released as the first release on my own Lamplight Records label.

However, after the routine of *Mutiny* I was anxious to get back to my music, so Mel Bush put together an extensive tour of fifty dates and in the autumn of 1987 I was back on another sell-out tour.

A month or so before the tour started Carlotta broke the unexpected news that she was pregnant. This revelation filled me with a mixture of feelings: part of me was thrilled by the prospect, but I was worried how Verity and Danny, my two children with Maureen, would react.

Carlotta suggested she should perhaps return to her family in America to have the baby and that we gauge the reaction as time went on. This was a typically unselfish response by Carlotta who over the years had become very close to the children, Danny especially, and would never do anything to upset my previous family. For me the chance to let the dust settle seemed a good idea, so as I went on tour, Carlotta went home to Rhode Island.

After the tour finished, Christmas was on the horizon. I knew it was my duty to spill the beans to Verity and Dan and reassure them that they wouldn't be losing a dad but gaining a brother or a sister. I decided to wait till after Christmas, and it was just as well I did. In fact it was just after New Year when the phone rang.

'Are you sitting down?' Carlotta said. 'It's twins.'

'No!' was my amazed reply, followed by 'Right.'

Now this was something. In Africa the father of twins is thought of as something very special, and I must say I felt like that myself.

I also hoped the fact that there were two babies would soften the news for Verity and Dan, and I think it did. Dan seemed to think it was cool, although Verity was a little worried and upset. But as the years moved on the love that's grown between my four children is truly wonderful.

With confirmation from across the Atlantic that twins were on the way, we still had no idea if they were boys or girls or in fact one of each. It was on a trip to visit Carlotta, who was fast becoming as wide as she was tall, that we went together to the hospital for a check on the babies' wellbeing and were told they were boys.

I was very happy, and the fact they were boys I think reassured Verity. She knew she was still her daddy's only girl.

When I arrived home my assistant Madge had a pile of messages for me, including one from a respected BBC drama producer named Susie Belbin. It seemed interesting, so Mel set up a meeting at Television Centre. At the appointed hour we were shown through to a boardroom, where coffee and sandwiches were laid on.

Susie, a lovely lady with a husky voice, asked if I would be interested in starring in a situation comedy they were developing. At first I had some reservations. Under Derek's brilliant influence over the years we had always been a little careful about the common denominator that popular TV seems to dumb down to. In recent years with 'reality' programmes like *Big Brother*, TV seems to have gone from dumb down to dumber down. So taking part in a sitcom was not high on the list of my career ambitions.

The meeting was a good one, though, and I liked Susie. So, taking the first draft scripts of the proposed series with me, I promised to read them, give the project some thought, and let her know if I was up for doing it. When I got round to reading the scripts I thought they were a little different to the run-of-the-mill sitcoms, being humorous and gentle. My character, Davey, had an appealing philosophy. He was a lock-keeper with a love of nature, almost gypsy-like. It was little wonder that I had been considered for the role, as Davey was pretty close to David. Mel was all for doing it, and even Derek was not as disapproving as I might have imagined, so I decided to take a chance and say yes.

It was agreed that I would write the music for the show and the title was changed at my suggestion from *The Lock-keeper* to *The River*. The next job was to find a leading lady. Susie had lined up three actresses for me to meet and was anxious to know which of them I felt would be right. To be honest all three were, but somehow Kate Murphy seemed to have the edge. A Scottish actress with a wonderful quality and a natural sense of comedy, strong yet vulnerable, Katy was our choice.

With the two main players in place, I started to think about writing a song for *The River*. In fact I was sitting at the piano trying to touch that ghost very late at night on 19 May 1988 when the phone rang. It surprised me as thankfully I rarely get calls late at night. My mind immediately went to America and Carlotta and, sure enough, it was a call to tell me that Carlotta had gone into labour prematurely and had been admitted to a maternity hospital in Rhode Island.

I thanked the caller, a close relation, and said, 'I'm on my way' – all very decisive, but not so easy to organize at one o'clock in the morning. Needless to say I didn't sleep, and as the sun rose over London, I headed for Heathrow.

The first plane I could get to Boston landed about five in the afternoon US time. Waiting for me at the airport was a family friend, Jim. I thanked him for picking me up and nervously asked about progress. It seemed that just as the plane made its final approach two tiny boys were born. I regretted not having been there for their arrival but was relieved that Carlotta and the twins were OK.

We drove for two hours to the hospital, and when we got there

I ran through the labyrinth of corridors to find Carlotta. As every mother will know, giving birth is not the easiest experience, and having two babies was even more painful. When I saw her I could tell she had suffered, but her thoughts were firmly on the welfare of the babies, who were both in intensive care.

A chill ran through me.

'Can I see them?'

'Of course,' said a sympathetic nurse who led me to the Intensive Care Unit. When I walked in there were seven or eight babies in plastic-covered cribs being attended to by a host of medics. I was taken to the far end of the room and there they were, so tiny, the elder twin weighing three pounds fifteen ounces and the younger (by fifteen minutes) weighing just one ounce less. My heart went out to them as I saw the drips and what seemed to be dozens of other leads and tubes attached to their tiny hands, feet and noses. They looked so helpless and in pain from the gadgets that had been stuck into them, and so sweet with little woollen hats on their heads to keep them warm.

I turned to a doctor monitoring another baby close by.

'Will they be all right?' My voice trembled.

'It's a little early to tell,' came a worrying reply.

I just stood and looked at them. As every parent knows, if your child is hurting or in danger, the pain and concern you feel is incredibly intense. As I stood there a nurse stuck yet another needle and tube into one of my little sons, who cried out in pain. I actually felt like hitting her but managed to contain myself.

'Will they be all right?' I asked again.

The nurse turned to me and said, 'Of course they will. It's not unusual for twins to be premature and underweight. Now don't you worry.'

'Thank you,' I said as my feelings changed from wanting to hit her to wanting to hug her.

As the days passed the boys and their mother gradually got

stronger. We decided to name them Kit and Bill, and two weeks or so after they were born, Carlotta was allowed to leave the hospital and we were finally able to bring them back to the loving environment of their Italian-American grandparents. What a fuss was made of them.

After a week or so, knowing now the boys were safe and happy, I flew back to London and started filming *The River*.

A terrific cast had been assembled and we headed for our fictional location of Chumley-on-the-Water. A very picturesque lock-keeper's cottage would be the centre of all the exterior filming. Although in pictures the river looked idyllic, in truth it was pretty stagnant and a directive had come from the BBC that for health reasons, if anyone jumped in, every orifice should be protected from germs – difficult. All the interior filming took place in the TV studio with an invited audience.

For the outside filming, a piglet was part of my character's menagerie. The only trouble was that piglets grow so fast ours had to be replaced three times as each pig outgrew its part.

Susie and the cast were wonderful. I can't tell you how many times the acting broke down in a fit of giggles. *The River* was a lot of fun, and its gentle pace and comedy was warmly received – it was regularly watched by over thirteen million households every week of its six-week run.

Although there were preliminary talks about another series, one was enough for me. I finished work on the series and went back to America, bought a house in Connecticut as a more permanent base for Carlotta and the boys and rounded off 1988 back in London finishing the *Touching the Ghost* album.

A lot of 1989 I spent travelling back and forth to America. I was offered an American TV show but turned it down. I liked the script, but the contract they wanted me to sign was for ever and a day, so I said no. However, it seemed that the more I said no, the more they wanted me to do it, till finally they were camped outside my house in Connecticut offering drugs, girls, anything. I stuck to my guns, though, and came back to England to do the Royal Variety Show.

It is a great honour to be asked to do the Royal Variety Show and I have in fact done it twice. You may also not know that I was the first ever commoner to turn on the Christmas lights in Regent Street. What about that?

Anyway it was nice to be asked to do the Royal Variety, but to be honest I didn't enjoy the experience. Sadly the edge was taken off for me by all the backstage egos and arguments. Who's top of the bill? How long do I get? I'd like a bigger dressing-room. I was just kind of happy to be there.

I've had mixed feelings too about the Children in Need annual TV event. Of course the cause is brilliant, totally worthy, and the generosity of the British Public is awesome, but as for all the wheeling and dealing that goes on as people try to plug whatever they are selling, secure the right time slot or make sure their appearance is national and not just regional – that's not what I thought it was about. Now I just send a cheque.

I understand that it's important to give aid where it is needed and sometimes to publicize needy causes, but I think there should be a completely selfless approach. The idea of using a charity to publicize what a good person you are I feel is very wrong, so I reacted with some trepidation when Voluntary Service Overseas approached me to become their Ambassador of the Year.

# 23

# Under Different Skies

I received a letter and a complete outline of the VSO's aims and admirable work from a man called Dick Rowe. I was honoured to be approached as a prospective Ambassador, so Madge fixed up a meeting. I immediately liked Dick very much. He was a positive and kind man who radiated a real warmth. My job as Ambassador would be to try and publicize VSO and the good work it does. I believed in it and wanted to do it, but my worry was that the media would think I was doing it to enhance my career. I told Dick that I was honoured to be asked and would give him an answer when I'd thought it through.

I decided to say yes, and an official handover reception was soon arranged. The previous Ambassador had been Lord Lichfield, so the venue was to be his photographic studio in North London.

It was a fascinating gathering. There seemed to be dignitaries there from every developing country in the world. Speeches were made, photos taken, interviews done and I was enrolled as VSO's 1990 Ambassador of the Year, a distinct improvement on Rear of the Year.

From the outset I had said to the head of VSO David Greene and to Dick Rowe that I didn't want to be just a name on their headed paper. I wanted to be involved in their work. For those who don't know about it, VSO sends people to the Developing World to pass on their particular skills to local counterparts, usually for a two-year period. It's a very grassroots and effective way of helping people to help themselves.

It was soon time for my first trip to meet Volunteers and see their work at first hand. Dick rang me and said, 'How does a trip to Uganda sound?'

'Good,' I replied and within a few weeks, rattling with malaria tablets and injected with every vaccine known to the medical world, Dick and I took off for Entebbe.

My knowledge of Uganda was pretty limited. I had read the horror stories surrounding the Idi Amin regime and remembered Entebbe Airport being blown up in some terrorist skirmish, but apart from that I knew very little. Dick, who was a brilliant travelling companion, did his best to brief me on Uganda's difficult recent history. Once described as 'the Pearl of Africa', it had been battered and bruised by civil war and tribal conflict and sadly, like many countries in the African continent, it was ravaged by AIDS. We spoke of the Volunteers and their respective projects and after a couple of stops in places I had never heard of, we landed at Entebbe.

The warm air and the warmth of the people hit me immediately. It was the beginning of my love affair with the country. We were met by a wonderful man called John. John was the Field Officer in Uganda and would be our guide during the two-week trip. We shook hands and were led out of the bustling airport to a jeep in the car park.

Kampala was full of life as we drove through the capital in the early evening. The street markets were in full flow and it seemed everybody was selling something; the bumpy roads were filled with bikes, scooters, battered cars, and overloaded and ancient buses; and women and girls carried impossible loads balanced on their heads.

Still visible was the war damage suffered in recent battles. Asian names could be seen painted on derelict shops, which were little more than concrete sheds. Africans had taken over, although one could still see a small Asian presence surviving and doing business long after Amin's cruel purge.

As we drove out to the suburbs of Kampala *en route* to the compound which would be our base, I was struck by how lush and green it all looked. For some reason I had expected it to be dry and dusty, but here was a fertile and beautiful country. John soon brought me down to earth as he explained that he was a recent arrival in Uganda himself, having been posted there a few months back after the previous Field Officer had been murdered for petrol in the very same compound where we were staying. Not much was said after that, and the three of us did what we could to avoid broken bones as we bounced along the bumpy roads.

The compound was surrounded by a high tin fence guarded by a sleepy African gentleman who had a big stick and an ill-fitting uniform. With a drowsy salute he opened the gates, and we drove in.

The house, a kind of bungalow, was pleasant and surrounded by a beautiful garden. Inside it was Spartan but comfortable. John showed us our rooms and we dropped off our bags. My room had a small double bed covered with a mosquito net, a chair and a wardrobe. With an early start promised, we hit the sack.

The next morning I was up early, we drank coffee and discussed the itinerary. There were farms, schools and centres to visit and many rough miles to cover. I was looking forward to seeing both the Volunteers and their projects, and Uganda and its people.

As we loaded the truck and drove away from the compound I was struck by the redness of the earth and the bright colours of flowers that poked their heads through the dark green of the plants and trees. Life was already in full swing, with people shopping for maize or bread, water being carried on heads, and those children that were lucky enough making their way to school.

Our first scheduled stop was at a Teacher Training College in a place called Nkozi, about an hour and a half away from Kampala. There were two young VSO teachers working there whom we were planning to visit. For most of the journey the road was good, much of it built by the Chinese as a gesture of friendship, and another bit by Cuba. All too soon, however, it came to an end and the last hour was spent bouncing through massive craters along dusty roads.

Finally we came to the college. It was a sprawling campus dotted with a mixture of mud huts, brick and tin buildings and gardens which were strangely quiet. Sadly our visit had coincided with the trainee teachers' holidays, but the principal was there and the two teachers, John and Sheila. They were terrific people, totally committed to their work. We toured the campus and heard their wishes and hopes. To my surprise as we walked around the semi-deserted buildings the principal showed me a building with a raised concrete stage which he called the theatre. It seemed that the college had a music and drama department. Knowing that I was an actor or something, he asked if I would come and teach there.

'If I can I would like to,' I replied. We had some bananas and tea for lunch and continued on our way.

Over the two-week period we travelled and saw a great deal of the good work that VSO was doing in this wonderful country. Some of the things we saw were disturbing, but because of the dedication of the Volunteers I always came away with hope.

One trip we made was to see a young Volunteer called Mary who was working in a compound for orphaned children. The moment I walked in, one boy slightly older than the other children gave me the biggest smile and hug. I spent the rest of the visit carrying him piggyback as he refused to leave me. The children in the compound were in various states of mind. Some had been found wandering in the bush, their parents killed in civil strife; others had been orphaned when their parents had died of AIDS; some sat in corners so traumatized they did not communicate; others smiled happily. Mary and her two Ugandan helpers were saint-like. Mary showed me proudly some children sitting in a circle, gently passing to each other some bottle tops on a string, a toy that she had made for them. Helping these children to relate to others was important, of course, as they had retreated into a world of their own, unable to face the reality of their tragic history. Here and now they were starting to communicate with each other.

When you see situations and people like that you feel humble. In fact, the overriding thing that was said to me by Volunteers was, 'We came to teach but we learned so much.'

In the busy central market in Kampala I met an impressive young girl who had left a high-flying job in the financial houses of New York and organized a group of lepers into a co-operative. Before her initiative the lepers would simply beg for money. Now they were proud stall-holders selling small items and making a modest profit.

The heads of the co-op even had a little office which they had made from cardboard boxes, and I was invited in to sign their visitors' book – the protocol runs very deep in Africa. As I shook hands with all of them, ignoring the damage this terrible disease leprosy had done, the total pride they had in their new existence was wonderful to see.

I also met a middle-aged ex-headmistress of a big comprehensive school in Birmingham who worked in a rural part of Uganda, tearing around on a motorbike in between her bouts of malaria. She had not only gained the respect of the women but also the men, as she worked for women's rights and did her best to help AIDS sufferers.

On one visit, I met a village chief who had recently benefited from the work of VSO engineers. They had helped build a water standpipe for the village, and had also ensured that the dangerous well had been made safe. This was of prime and personal importance to the chief, because as a little boy he himself had fallen into one of these wells and nearly drowned.

The chief was so pleased, he seemed to think I was a saviour. In fact when we left he insisted on giving me a live chicken and, I think, one of his wives. I was about to refuse both when a Volunteer's voice whispered in my ear, 'I'll have the chicken.' Wages for a Volunteer are pretty meagre, so away we went with a live chicken under my arm, but not hand in hand with the wife.

So many pictures and experiences filled my head as we finally left Uganda. Dick, or Phineas Fogg as I had started to call him, was now a close friend. As we boarded the plane at Entebbe he asked me whether I would like to come back someday.

'I'd love to. Perhaps I'll take up that offer at Nkozi,' I replied. He laughed, but somehow I think both of us knew that I would return.

With the human emotions I'd felt in Africa still running deep, England at first seemed a little like a foreign land. My perspective had changed, and I couldn't help questioning the selfish materialism I was seeing more clearly than ever. So much around us seemed excessive. To see the basic level at which so many of the Ugandans managed to exist, in poverty and poor conditions, yet with optimism and happiness, had been very inspiring.

Offers from the less real world of showbiz had been floating by in my absence. One unusual one came from a Japanese film company, asking me to play an evil Spanish duke in Yugoslavia. It seemed too silly an opportunity to miss. I flew to Hollywood to meet the star of the movie and one of the producers, 'Ninja' himself, Sho Kosugi. My son Dan was really impressed as this man was a martial arts legend. Sho had heard about my performance as Che and offered me the part of Don Pedro. Half of the film was to be shot in Japan and the other in Yugoslavia. I read the script, and as I fancied playing a bad guy for a change I signed up for *Shogun Mayeda*.

My parts of the filming were based in Yugoslavia, so at the given time I flew to Belgrade. We filmed in Dubrovnik, Belgrade and Montenegro. They are all beautiful places, although I found Montenegro, which is near Albania, a little weird. It was there that I saw a gypsy with a dancing bear. The poor bear wasn't so much dancing as trying to avoid the pain it must have felt as its handler cruelly manoeuvred a great hook that had been put through the bear's lip. Disgusting.

I was there in 1992 just before the terrible ethnic wars that tore the country apart, but even then there was a tension in the air. You could feel the mutual suspicion and contempt even within the film unit.

Sho was a famous martial arts guy, so it was obvious this was going to be a pretty physical film. The fight co-ordinators were Japanese and spoke absolutely no English, so as they taught me the fights we developed a whole new language to describe the moves.

This sounded like it was straight out of a comic book, with words like 'Ka-Boom' or 'Whooosh'. You could often see me enquiring if it was a 'Ka-Boom' or a 'Whooosh' as we staged the epic.

Christopher Lee, the famous Dracula, was in the film with me and was most kind when an accident happened that almost cost me the sight of my right eye. We were filming yet another action sequence which required us, the Spanish, to fire muskets at them, the Japanese. I should have known that things could get sticky when I saw the special effects man, who was responsible for safety with guns, covered in bandages and burns which he sustained whilst half blowing himself up.

After we had shot our guns once at the imaginary enemy, the director decided to do another take. The bandaged FX man, a giant Serb, refilled my gun with gunpowder but must have been a bit generous, for when the order to fire came, my gun went off like a cannon, blowing back and shooting gunpowder and flint into my eye.

It felt as if a hot needle had pierced my eye, but reacting in the same way as most actors, I said I was fine and ready to keep going. At this point Christopher Lee stepped in and demanded that I should be taken to hospital, and with a look of inconvenience the director eventually agreed. So off I went to the hospital with an interpreter and a sore eye. When we got there, the hospital was closed for a holiday or something, so away we went to find another one. It didn't seem promising.

The second hospital was open, and we went in and were ushered into a waiting room. Soon, probably quicker than under the National Health, a white-coated doctor came out to see me. As the interpreter explained what had happened, Doc took a look.

After their brief conversation the interpreter turned to me and said, 'The doctor says he must operate immediately.'

'Right,' I replied and dutifully followed the doctor into a basic operating room. The room housed a bed with some surgical stuff littered around. I sat down on the bed, and the doctor left the room. Soon a middle-aged nurse came in, smiled and started washing some bits in a sink – all very hygienic, except for the cigarette in her mouth. My mind started to sum up the situation. Here I was in the second choice hospital in a nearly third world country, the nurse is having a fag and a doctor who doesn't speak my language is about to operate on my eye. 'I wonder?' I thought.

The doctor came back, my nurse put the fag out and they gestured for me to lie back. Holding my eye open, in he came with a scalpel, which looked to me like a broadsword. He then cut into my eye and started to scrape and dig about. Now without any anaesthetic at all, this wasn't comfortable.

After a few minutes and an 'everything is all right' type of smile, in came the nurse to administer stitches. Using what looked like lengths of rope, she sewed up my eye. I thanked them both and the interpreter and I drove back to the location hotel.

My immediate thought as I reflected on the day's events was that I should get back to England and get this eye thing checked out. The next morning I met with the director and it was obvious that filming was out of the question for me for the time being, as the eye was red and some minor swelling had developed. He suggested I took a week off and went back to have it looked at. The following day I boarded the plane and flew in to London.

At the airport there were scores of photographers and press, and even TV news cameras were there to meet the wounded pop star. The coverage was a little sensational, but it was nice to known they cared.

I managed to get an appointment in the morning with an eminent eye specialist called Eric Arnott, and after a pretty uncomfortable night I travelled to Harley Street.

Eric came into the room, an impressive man with a bow tie who had done much to help cataract sufferers in the Developing World. I told him what had happened and he began to examine me.

'Well, whoever did this did a brilliant job,' he said, much to my relief. 'I guarantee, when the stitches are taken out the scar will be virtually invisible.' Eric then went on to explain why the Yugoslav doctor was in such a hurry to operate. Apparently gunpowder is a corrosive that would have eaten my eye away in a very short time, leaving me blind, so there was definitely a degree of urgency to his actions.

I decided that on my return to Belgrade I would take a bottle of whisky to thank the doctor with, and of course a packet of fags for the nurse.

After a week or so I was back doing the 'Ka-boom' and 'Whooosh' stuff. You know those Japanese endurance shows? Well I was starting to feel like a contestant. The big moment for my character Don Pedro was when he got his come-uppance by being sliced in two after a fierce battle with Sho, the Samurai warrior. This was to take place in some fast-flowing rapids – sounds cool, doesn't it?

I decided to do the stunt myself, which meant I had to clunk, 'Ka-boom' and 'Whoosh' around in a suit of armour, in a fast-flowing river. I would crash into the rapids, bouncing over a few rocks, but I'd be protected by my armour – Yeah. Hopefully the splitting of me into two parts would be a special effect.

The Japanese fight guys had strung ropes across the river bank for me to grab on to. After a pretty impressive sword fight, it was my time to die, so I fell back like a giant discarded tin can. As the rapids took me down river, I went bang crash wallop over the rocks before finally grabbing my last-chance strategically positioned rope, and was hauled in wet and rusting to the river bank. This was followed by a smiling round of applause from the Japanese and a smile of relief from me.

The applauding Japanese reminded me of a trip I'd made in the Seventies to a record company in a building with sixteen floors. I was positioned in a lift and at each floor my host would stop the lift, whereupon the workforce would applaud for about five minutes, and on we would go to the next floor and the next lot of dedicated workers.

All in all it was definitely an unusual film to make, but I enjoyed the change and I understand the film was very big in Japan.

Although I had been absorbed with Don Pedro versus the Japanese, my thoughts were very much with Uganda and VSO, and I was soon pleased to hear that the college in Uganda had made an official request for me to come and teach. I agreed formally and we decided we would talk about the timing of my visit at a later date. I also approached the VSO with a fund-raising idea on the music front.

My idea was to record musicians in some of the many countries the VSO were in – forty-eight at the time – and compile an album. To keep costs down, I also approached the wonderful Peter Gabriel, and Amanda Jones who ran his WOMAD record label, which had a history of recording Developing World musicians. They, and the fine record label Ace run by Ben Mandleson and Roger Armstrong, were really helpful and generous to the project.

With the enthusiastic agreement of the VSO I began to plan the difficult logistics of the recording. It was agreed that I would go to Uganda, Belize and parts of the Caribbean. It was a fascinating and exciting prospect, but in many ways I was winging it. I would be visiting Volunteers and their projects, and in the process I would enquire about local musicians, try to round them up and listen to them. If I liked what I heard I would then try to find a facility to record them. In retrospect things came together surprisingly well. I found a man in St Lucia called Boo Hinkson singing calypso in a hotel and later recorded a terrific track in Boo's home studio called 'Calypso Classic'. I wondered where Boo had got his nickname from but didn't like to ask. I was graphically shown one day while walking in St Lucia when a cat crossed our path and Boo literally jumped into my arms.

I did the bulk of my recording in Uganda in a studio just outside Kampala called Sunrise, a small place used mainly for Christian programmes. The biggest band in Uganda, called Afrigo, kindly came to record for me. There were also more traditional musicians like Dr Semke and Abolugana Kagalana, who were fantastic to record. To everyone's surprise they were a day too early when they turned up from the bush, along with their group of musicians and some weird and wonderful instruments, so I had to organize some food and a bed for the night. The guys finished up sleeping in the studio, but at least we got an early start.

It was marvellous to see the reaction of these men when they heard themselves back for the first time, it made everything seem worthwhile. I suppose it's like any job, however glamorous it may seem – we can all do with a fresh perspective. I have been involved in music for a long time and it's all too easy to take things for granted. Seeing the raw joy of these musicians hearing themselves and their music for the first time was a pleasant reminder of why I became a musician.

At the end of my travels I brought the tapes back to England for overdubbing and mixing. I decided that in order to boost the commercial prospects of the CD I should perhaps write a song as a little tribute to Africa and include it on the album. I was lucky to obtain the services of the brilliant South African girls Shikisha, and African guitarist Abdul Tee-Jay and with the help of Ian Wherry we produced 'Africa – You Shine'. You can't say this wasn't a well travelled album – I even went to Sheffield to record some Indian musicians called Chhayanot at the Axis studio.

The finished work came out in 1991 and I called it *Under Different Skies*. Sadly, like most world music albums it did not get the sales or exposure I think it deserved, but because of the constant support of so many people who have related to what I've done over the years, it made money for both the poor musicians and for VSO.

# 24

# Shipwrecked

Over the previous years I had been approached to re-enter Panto Land, but the memory of the kissing bear and, even worse, the dancing one lingered long. Besides, the scripts I had been sent were quite honestly lousy. But I do feel that the pantomime format is an important one, for this reason. It's as a child that most people go into a theatre and sample the wonders of a live production for the first time, and usually it's to see a pantomime. If what they see on that first visit is something worthwhile, if they have the right initiation, then they are more likely to go to the theatre in future years. With this in mind I started to think about writing my own pantomime.

I fixed on the story of Robinson Crusoe and dutifully read the original book by Daniel Defoe. Strange that I seem to be drawn to subject-matter about boats, especially as I don't like them and most of my experiences with real live boats have ended in near disaster.

Anyway after reading it, I thought this may have been a fantastic book for children of earlier generations, with its adventures on a far away desert island but today, with the world a much smaller place, a few liberties needed to be taken with the story-line.

I teamed up with the brilliant director Robin Midgley and friend and writer David Joss Buckley and we came up with a story-line filled with magic and hexes, and an overall theme of good against evil. It was important to all of us, I think, that the character of Man Friday was treated with respect and dignity. I remember seeing one awful version of *Robinson Crusoe* where all he seemed to do was jump up and down in a monkey suit.

We approached the show as we would any musical. I wrote specific music for it and, where it worked, included some of the score from *Mutiny*. Robin and David did a great job writing up the story-line we had developed, and after another UK concert tour I went headlong into rehearsals.

The rehearsals had a terrific buzz about them. Winkle, played by Micky O'Donoughue, and Red Beard, played by John Labanowski, were truly inspired and very funny. They brought madness and anarchy to the piece – and to the rehearsals. Although we had approached the show like a musical, we also included some classic pantomime themes. No women dressed as men, but a wonderful Dame played by the equally wonderful Bobby Bennett, who by the way ain't a bad footballer. All in all we had assembled a superb cast, including my own daughter Verity, who was cast by Robin to play my daughter in the show.

We opened at the Alhambra theatre in Bradford to excellent reviews and broke all their box-office records. In the show there are parts for children to play, and a group of young performers called the Bradford Sunbeams were wonderful as they strutted like peacocks or bounced like monkeys. A real credit to the Sunbeams' reputation.

It was great to work with Verity and I was proud to see her doing so well. Her voice was terrific and her performance surprised me with its professionalism. Over the years since I have often been away from home over Christmas doing the show and have spent the day with the dear friends I've made in the cast. I remember one occasion in Edinburgh when Red Beard decided he would cook Christmas dinner for us, at my rented flat, which he did beautifully until he got the turkey out of the oven and accidentally dropped it into the sink. Poor John was so enraged that he had to be physically restrained from attacking the turkey and ripping it to pieces. Micky, Bobby, John, David and Robin are like family now and I think the world of them.

By the end of the run I was feeling pretty whacked, having come straight into *Crusoe* from a lengthy rock tour. I needed a lot of energy for the show, but seeing the children in the audience, not to mention the mums and dads living the show, was a wonderful reward and helped me through it.

When I got back to London, Dick Rowe called and we fixed a date for my teaching trip to Uganda. I had been thinking a lot about what I would work at with the student teachers and had decided to attempt a version of the musical *Godspell*. After all I knew it well, and being so simple to produce it could be staged anywhere with the most limited resources. Even in the London production the set and props for my crucifixion were a beer crate and two red ribbons.

I got hold of some T-shirts for costumes and some magic tricks for Jesus, but I knew I needed a pianist to take with me. I asked Ian Wherry, but he couldn't do it. Then I had a brainwave. I had met a talented musician and accompanist called Helen Ireland at some of the *Robinson Crusoe* auditions. I thought she was terrific, so I gave her a call to see if she fancied a couple of months in rural Uganda.

After her initial shock Helen thankfully said yes. I'm so glad she did. I doubt if I could have managed without her care and energy. We flew out together, and I talked about my attitude and ideas for the show. Soon we landed at Entebbe. There to meet us was a new VSO Field Officer who took us by jeep to what would be our home for the next few weeks.

We arrived at the campus in the dark, but stars and a big yellow moon threw a soft light on the scene. There were small groups of students talking and laughing, and someone playing a traditional drum. We were welcomed and led to a row of tin shacks where the teachers lived. There were three of them. Helen and I were to share the middle one, and our neighbours on one side were friends John and Sheila, and on the other a Ugandan teacher who would be my assistant, a man called Celestine.

We went in and Celestine lit a candle. There was a small lounge, two small bedrooms and a kitchen and bathroom – luxury in this part of the world. Also, Celestine said, sometimes the electricity came on. Helen and I fumbled around in the dark, picked our rooms and tried to make ourselves at home.

I was just drifting off to sleep when I heard a muffled scream from Helen's bedroom. Freeing myself from the mosquito net I jumped out of bed, but as I put my bare feet down on the floor I heard a crunching sound and felt a sort of squishing feeling between my toes. After scrabbling about for the candle and the matches I discovered that this strange sensation was my bare feet stepping on a moving carpet of giant cockroaches. As the light shone from the candle, my room-mates started to melt away – as Arthur Askey would say, before your very eyes. I stood slightly bemused, with cockroach bits between my toes, watching the exodus, then gingerly tiptoed to Helen's room. Helen was trying to be brave but was not too keen on our visitors. As time went on, however, we and they seemed to accept each other and lived happily side by side.

The next morning I woke with the sunrise, got out from under my mosquito net and looked out of the window. Dotted around us were a few mud huts with families already busy fetching water or cooking breakfast over an open fire. There was a sweet smell of burning logs that floated on the crisp morning air. Green trees and soft hills rolled off into the horizon. You could hear the sound of goats, strange birds and animals noises. It was beautiful and it was Africa.

Celestine had kindly brought us a can of water from the well, so Helen and I got washed in readiness to meet our new students.

Walking through a cluster of mud huts and smiling faces, I was feeling apprehensive as we made our way to the theatre, which I had seen on my previous visit: a tin-roofed brick building with a concrete raised platform at one end – the stage.

There waiting for us and singing a wonderful welcome song were our thirty-six trainee teachers. There seemed to be more or less an equal number of boys and girls, and their average age was about twenty-three.

How welcome they made us feel, and how enthusiastic they were about the prospect of learning. I thanked them for their welcome and introduced Helen. Next I briefly outlined my intention of staging a musical, which received an enthusiastic response, although it's fair to assume that not one of them had ever seen a musical, so there was much work to do.

The first job was to cast it, so a succession of quick auditions was organized. Celestine had managed to borrow a piano from a local church, and we worked with our prospective cast one by one.

Generally the standard for amateurs was good. My idea was to cast the ten clowns, including Jesus, and to beef up the singing I'd use the rest of the twenty-six as a kind of Greek chorus.

Everybody wanted to play Jesus, even the girls, but finally I decided on a boy whose name was David. I chose the other nine principals and ten understudies. I liked the idea of a black Jesus and was confident that the boy I chose could do it well. As for Judas, the boy selected for that had terrific potential, and at the end of the first day I was confident that we could make it happen.

Tired but absorbed by our first working day, Helen and I went back to our tin shack. I cooked dinner, which became a regular event as Helen, although she is a terrific musician, is not that hot in the kitchen. Well, that was her excuse anyway, so a routine started to unfold – I did most of the cooking and Helen did the washing-up.

The small battery radio I had brought with me was good company and the BBC World Service became a lifeline. As Celestine promised, the electricity did come on a couple of times, but we had a good stock of candles so we made the best of it.

One night when the inconsistent electricity had sparked into life, I thought I would leave our outside light on, so that the family close by could have some light. About three in the morning the sound of voices and laughter woke me up. Turning on the under-used bedroom light to disperse my room-mates, I took a look outside and discovered our neighbours gathered around our outside light, feasting on the flying ants that had been attracted to it. Now flying ants may not sound that great to you and me, but for the villagers they were a good source of protein and quite a treat.

Over the days and weeks Helen worked tirelessly to teach our willing cast the music from the show, and as the songs unfolded, memories of my *Godspell* days and my distant friends would flood back. It was very emotive as the students started to grow more and more in confidence, and became familiar with the music and the harmonies. It soon became apparent that the Africans were natural story-tellers and performers; in fact my task in most cases was to make the acting smaller and more realistic. We had a lot of fun, but we worked long and hard to move forward.

A local carpenter made me the set from an old table, consisting of two saw horses and three planks, and a plastic bottle crate was found at the local store. Some ladies in the village helped with the costumes, and slowly but surely the show started to take shape. I would take other workshops to relieve the pressure and, when we could, I coached and organized some football sessions using some footballs that West Ham had kindly donated for the trip.

The spirit of togetherness was crucial, and as we moved

towards our proposed opening date we were more or less ready. The plan was to open first at the Nkozi College, play there for three performances, move on to play another college and then to the big time – the National Theatre in Kampala.

All was set for the opening show. Nuns and some Cuban doctors were invited from a local hospital, people came from the surrounding villages, and VSO Volunteers from local projects all arrived for the show.

The first show was a triumph, and I was so proud of my cast. Just as in London all those years ago, the audience were moved to tears by the simple crucifixion at the end of the show. Their honest reaction to all the hard work we had put in was really rewarding. There was one sticky moment when a goat decided to wander in and join us, causing quite a stir as he baa'd and butted his way through my Greek chorus, but just like true showbiz professionals they carried on regardless. With the triumph of our opening, the cast were loving it and it was time to get the show on the road.

I had arranged to hire a truck to transport us and our simple set to the college for our next date. The truck was to pick us up at noon, so that we could get to the venue in good time, get in and set up for an evening performance. This place apparently had electricity and lights.

In Africa time keeping does not have the importance that it has for us Europeans. For instance, if a man says he will meet you at noon he could well turn up at three in the afternoon or even the next day. It takes a bit of getting used to, but if he is on his way to you and he meets a friend he will hang out with them for a while and leave when he feels like it. Of course, if he gets waylaid by someone else, who knows when he'll turn up! So the fact that by 1.30 our truck had not turned up was kind of usual. By two o'clock I was looking for an answer. Celestine went to the hospital to try and phone for an estimated time of arrival. When he returned he had news that the truck had broken down and would not be coming.

'Right,' I said, a little like an Army officer, 'is there another truck we could contact?'

'Not that I know of,' came Celestine's reply.

I left the cast playing football and took the jeep into Nkozi town to search for some transport. As I drove around, I spotted some builders emptying sand from a rather beaten-up truck. I pulled over and went up to them. 'I want to hire your truck,' I said. I think at first they thought this white bloke's bonkers, but as I persisted and explained the problem some chinks started to appear in the owner-driver's armour and, after some serious haggling, a deal was struck. I parked the jeep and headed off with a crash of gears in my rented truck.

In a cloud of black smoke I climbed the road back to the campus. As I trundled in, cheers rang out from the *Godspell* cast. We loaded up the piano, the set and our thirty-six students and drove to the outskirts of Kampala.

The venue was basically a school hall, but fair enough. There seemed to be rivalry between the two colleges, so my lot were determined to do well even though they were a little nervous. Two or three of them were suffering with bouts of malaria, and one of the girl principals was too ill to go on, so she was replaced by her understudy.

The hall was packed for the evening show, and did we show 'em? It seemed the cast had gone up another level. Both Jesus and Judas put in special performances and this seemed to radiate through the cast. I was especially pleased with the way the audience reacted, as they changed from indifference at the beginning to living every moment, laughing and crying in all the right places. Everyone was jubilant afterwards, and as we bedded down for the night in a borrowed dormitory, there was much excited talk of Kampala the next day – the big city, our next stop.

As day broke we were given a basic breakfast by our hosts and then began the mammoth task of getting Helen's piano back on the truck. Loaded and full of anticipation we trundled off to the National Theatre. I was told there would be a stage manager present to help me with lighting and sound and stuff. But when we arrived he was nowhere to be found. I made my way to the administrator's office, to be told that unfortunately our man had gone to a funeral and wouldn't be in today.

'Does he have an assistant?' I asked hopefully, but of course he didn't.

I went back to my waiting cast and we unloaded the truck. The piano seemed to be getting heavier and heavier. I found dressing-rooms for the boys and girls and set about trying to stage the show.

The National Theatre, although grand by name, was very basic. It did have a sound system and some stage lights, but with our man at a funeral it was a case of 'How does this work?' Celestine, Helen and I pushed buttons and fiddled with knobs and started to work out how to get things going. I found a big ladder and went up to set the lights, and slowly we progressed through a rather painful technical rehearsal.

The students were tired and restless, but they were patient, and slowly the show came together.

'Tonight is our biggest night yet,' I told them as I tried to focus not only the lights but also their tired minds. I was aware that I would have to work the lights, the sound and even the bar bells for our grand opening, and I tried to assure them that all would be well, but I must say I wasn't too confident.

By 6.30 the audience began to arrive for the seven o'clock show. This audience was a lot different from the ones we had played to. Here was a mixture of people from Consulates, various Aid organizations, thirty or so people from VSO and affluent and influential Ugandans. I told the cast not to be phased by a lack of response but just to believe in each other and keep doing what they had been doing so well. At seven I pushed the bar bells and the audience filed in.

There was an expectant buzz in the auditorium as John the Baptist made his way through the well-heeled audience to baptize Jesus. I had deliberately under-lit the opening so that when the clowns burst into 'Prepare Ye the Way of the Lord' there would be an explosion of light and colour. It worked, and from that moment the show seemed to take wing.

The audience loved it. I'm not sure how the individual performances were that night, as most of the time I was preoccupied, but the reaction at the end said it all. I was so proud of my students as they took their well-earned bows with the broadest smiles and a togetherness of spirit that you could not ignore. Everyone was a star, including dear Helen.

The congratulations rained down on them backstage, and the British Consulate invited us all back to their place to a reception in their honour. I looked on as my motley crew wandered the palatial grounds noshing the nibbles and drinking the Fanta. I'm sure it was an experience they would never forget – I know I won't.

With the success of the show we were asked to play there for a week. Funeral Man surfaced and I was able to sit and enjoy our last few shows. Helen and I had moved from cockroach city and were now based in the VSO compound with running water and electricity, and with shops in Kampala selling things like cheese, which we hadn't seen for weeks, we had a good last week.

I did nearly come unstuck, though. One day I was driving the jeep with a VSO Volunteer in the passenger seat, and in front of me was a jeep full of soldiers who manned the many armed checkpoints. They were going slowly, so I decided to overtake them, and as I pulled out to do so, up went their guns, all aimed at me. In a flash the Volunteer grabbed the wheel, turning our jeep ninety degrees on to a dirt road – and afterwards explained that if you overtake a military vehicle they shoot you.

With hearts full of memories, Helen and I prepared for the flight home. We travelled first back to our friends in Nkozi to say goodbye and later we were driven to the airport. The plane's take-off had been delayed, and as we waited patiently to board the plane, Helen said 'Look.' Around the perimeter fence were our students brandishing cardboard signs saying things like 'Come back soon' or 'We love you' and waving furiously. They had walked over twenty miles to be there to wish us a fond farewell.

I was deeply moved and felt privileged to have known them. I still receive the occasional letter from them. Most of them are teachers now, although one or two of the girls have become nuns. I'll always remember them, and the compliment paid to me by the boy who played Judas: 'You are a white man with an African soul.'

I made other trips with the VSO, but none probably as memorable as the Ugandan one. One time I was returning from a trip to Malawi and became really ill. I was all set to ignore it, but owing to the sensible intervention of Dick Rowe and Mel Bush I was taken against my will to the Hospital for Tropical Diseases and diagnosed with Tick Typhus fever. I was admitted and treated in a state of delirium which seemed to turn into a surreal comedy. This was because Mel had commissioned me to write the music for a Russian ice ballet company production of *Beauty and the Beast*, and a press and photo shoot had been fixed for the day after I had been admitted.

The date had been fixed for months at an ice rink in London. The Russians had flown in for it, and it was obviously important for Mel to publicize the forthcoming production. Not wanting to let anyone down, I agreed against doctors' orders to make an appearance.

In truth I wasn't really sure where I was at the time. I vaguely remember a big limo pulling up for me at this rather run-down hospital near Kings Cross, being taken to an ice rink, sliding around on some ice with some Amazon-like Russian skaters, trying to smile and going back to hospital. Fortunately, although the symptoms seemed to hit me hard, within a few days, thanks to expert care from Dr Peter Chynott, I was over it.

Without doubt my experience as Ambassador for VSO was very special to me, and today I am still a member of the council which decides VSO policy world-wide. The post of Ambassador of the Year had been so fruitful that it was extended to three years, and it was not until 1993 that I handed the torch to a new Ambassador, the Olympic gold medal athlete Fatima Whitbread.

For my next recording in 1993 I went into the studio with Mike Batt and the Royal Philharmonic Orchestra again, this time with a batch of songs by other writers that I fancied doing. Mike did a great job, and with the album *Cover Shot* I was back in the album charts at number three. Since the turn of the Nineties any new recordings I have made have been virtually ignored by every radio station in the country, so I remember waiting and listening to the Radio One Album Chart Show, confident at last that with a top-three album a track of mine would actually have to be played. When it came to the top of the chart the DJ named the album and the chart position but never played a track.

It's disappointing and frustrating as an artiste not to have your music played on the radio, as each year or so you present what you feel is good work. For me, I feel more disappointed and frustrated for the people that follow what I do, and thankfully there are thousands of them. Perhaps an even wider circle might relate to what I do if they got to hear my stuff. At least they could then make up their own minds if they wanted it or not. It's equally frustrating sometimes when a well-meaning member of the public asks if you are still making records, because he or she really likes your music – not easy to take, especially if you have just emerged from an all-night recording session. But I'll keep writing and recording as long as I feel I have something to say and as long as I feel there are people who are interested.

# 25

# Stooping to Conquer

In 1993 I was approached by Sir Peter Hall to return to the theatre in Oliver Goldsmith's classic *She Stoops to Conquer* – a challenge indeed, but you know me, I like a challenge.

We met, and the charismatic Don of Theatre gently persuaded me to play the part of Tony Lumpkin. Derek was all for me doing it, and I suspected the experience of working with Sir Peter would be valuable. But I was worried, as I had never attempted any of the classics, and the cast Sir Peter had assembled was formidable. A little against my instincts I agreed to do it.

Rehearsals started in mid summer with Sir Donald Sinden as Mr Hardcastle, my stepfather, and Miriam Margolyes as my mother, supported by a fine cast of fundamentally classical actors. I found the rehearsals nerve-racking. It was a new world for me, all very thespian, and I didn't feel too comfortable in it. I would be relieved when the day was done and I could hop on my Triumph Bonneville and cut loose in the warm summer evenings. Great things, motorbikes.

Miriam and the cast were very supportive and put in some wonderful performances, but I couldn't help feeling like an outsider. Sir Peter was the first director I had worked with who seemed always to be following the text and hardly ever watching the performances. It seemed the written word was paramount in his thoughts. With my lines learned and my hardly-watched performance more or less intact, we opened in Leatherhead, Surrey, and after a week there went on a tour of Britain. Houses were good and reviews were too. The plan was that if all went well on tour we would then take it into the West End, possibly at the end of the year.

In the course of the tour our performances had grown and settled. Donald and Miriam were getting laughs for their larger-than-life characterization, and audiences seemed to warm to them, as did the critics wherever we played.

I had a scene where I would throw Miriam over my shoulder and carry her off – rather a good exit. One night at the Festival Theatre, Chichester, with the rotund Miriam on my shoulder, I took a tumble, and unceremoniously dumped Miriam on a flight of stairs. Luckily she was unhurt, but I tore the ligaments in my ankle.

As luck would have it the accident happened just before our scheduled transfer to the Queen's Theatre in the West End, which meant I was forced to use a walking stick. Sir Peter had decided to rehearse us for our West End opening and strip away from the production many of the bits of stage business that had developed on the tour. I think he wanted to get back to the text in a more purist way. A little friction developed as things that Sir Peter felt were superfluous were removed from the performances. There were even discussions about whether I should wear a fat suit and a ginger wig. All of this panic was unsettling to the cast, and to cap it all on opening night I was very sick with food poisoning.

In retrospect I shouldn't really have gone on. The stage crew had kindly positioned buckets for me in various places, but it was as much as I could do to get through it. Needless to say, I didn't enjoy the opening at all. The personal reviews I got were poor, and the show's were not much better. Again it seemed I had stepped above my station and this was another chance to stick the knives in. We struggled on into the New Year.

Over the Christmas break I spent time with my family and my parents. Mum and Dad talked of moving a little closer to me as they were still in the wilds of Essex. We even started looking at suitable houses nearer to me.

Carlotta, Bill and Kit were now living in England and the boys were at school. The children were getting on well together by this time, and moving my parents closer would mean they could see their grandchildren more often. So it was with terrible irony that on Wednesday 24 January 1994 during the matinee performance I received a phone call from a hospital in Essex.

I was told my father had died.

Time stood still. I asked to speak to Mum and when she took the phone it was obvious she was in a state of shock. As we gently spoke she told me Dad had lunch, decided to take a short nap and when she tried to wake him he never woke up. I was devastated and my mind raced. What should I do? Leave the theatre and drive to the hospital? I tried to think what Dad would have done. I decided he would have gone on. After all, he had been so strong all his life, never giving up. I decided to finish the matinee and the evening show, then drive straight over to Mum's house and stay there. I then made sure that for the moment Mum was being taken care of and told her I would be there as soon as I finished the show. She seemed fine with that. I put the phone down and looked in the dressing-room mirror. I don't think the reality of what had happened had fully sunk in. I went and turned the tannoy up and heard the play moving to my next entrance. In a dream I walked to the stage and made my entrance, and as if on automatic pilot I finished the performance.

I never told the cast, the last thing I wanted was sympathy or pity. I wanted to be strong like my dad.

Between shows I walked through the streets of Soho. I don't even know what I did, but I seem to remember buying a coffee and being asked for an autograph which I signed in a detached way.

I was back in the Queen's Theatre by the 'half', which in theatre terms means the thirty-five minutes before the show starts, and as the clock ticked on I felt a power, an energy and a brightness inside of me. I can only say that that performance was the most powerful performance I have ever given. It was like an out-of-body experience. I know I connected with my father's spirit that night and the power was immense.

After the show I changed quickly and drove to Essex. Waves of sadness washed over me, but I knew I must focus on my mother. She had lost the one man in her life, someone she had known and loved for over sixty years.

I got to the house and Mum opened the door. I took her in my arms and hugged her. She looked just like the little girl who had met my dad all those years ago.

We talked well into the night, we laughed and we cried. The next morning I suggested that Mum came home with me. I told her to pack a few things, because she wouldn't be back for a while, and drove her back to stay at my place. From that day to this she has lived with us. I didn't want her living alone and there were too many memories for her to face day to day in the house they shared together.

Dad's funeral in London's East End was attended by all who knew him. A children's choir of little urchins from my primary school, Star Lane, sang as Dad's coffin was carried through the church, and the burial was as dignified as was my father.

As time passed the wounds were beginning to heal and Mum bravely started to try to rebuild her much-changed life. I was still doing *She Stoops to Conquer* when one night in February I turned into Soho Square as usual and there seemed to be an eerie silence. I saw two men crawling on the pavement in suits and ties, then out of nowhere this man jumped in front of my car, aimed a gun at me and ordered me out of the car, Now if I had been late and searching for a parking place, as I usually was, I would have gladly given him the car, but not tonight. Instead of giving him the car, I aimed it at him, caught him in the leg and drove off. As I went past, he fired a shot at the car, then another. I swerved quickly down the next turning and as I drove back round towards the theatre to park, I saw him again. This time he was running but with a limp.

I finally parked and walked to the stage door. By the time the interval came the stage door was packed with newspaper men, plus two plain-clothes policemen. I went out to talk to them. I told the police all I knew and tried to play down the incident to the press. Nevertheless the next morning's papers were full of 'Pop Star's Hijack Drama', etc. Thankfully a few days later the police informed me that the gunman had been arrested and charged.

Soon afterwards the play ended its run. It had not been the happiest time for me and I was relieved to leave.

It maybe on account of that experience that I became reluctant to commit to long theatre runs, although I have been asked. The commitment and routine of eight shows a week in the same thing, month in, month out, is a prospect I don't fancy any more unless, of course it was something that I thought was special. The short run of *Robinson Crusoe* at Christmas is more my cup of tea.

I suspect the reason I seem to be able to work in many mediums is because I do like change and find change a stimulant. That's why I enjoy the rock tours, I suppose. You are in a different city each night, and although there is a framework to the concert, each night in each venue is different. One of the regrets I have is that when I was younger my constant wish was to move on to tomorrow and not look back at yesterday. Which meant that I never savoured the considerable success I'd achieved. It was good in some ways, I suppose, as I certainly didn't rest on my laurels, but sad that I didn't feel pride in what I'd done.

Talking of change, musically I had a very interesting time in

1995, when I finally started working on the Russian ice ballet *Beauty and the Beast*. I had agreed to write the songs and score, and I persuaded Ian Wherry to arrange and produce it with me.

The writer David Wood came up with a story-line for the ballet, and I had lengthy and difficult conversations, through an interpreter, with the Russian lady choreographer. I suspect our minds wouldn't have met even if we had spoken the same language.

The songs were fine and included a couple of the strongest songs I've written, I think, but when it came to – and I quote – 'monkey up a rope' music Ian and I were sometimes at a loss. The length of dances kept chopping and changing. I suggested at the beginning that we should have a director to give us a sense of shape and oversee the production, but it was decided not to. Anyway, it was difficult, but we did it. In the last week of rehearsal before the Grand Gala opening at the Royal Albert Hall I never had time to sleep, as trying to finish the music was an ever-changing challenge.

Finally it was done and the day of the opening came. I thought it would be a big night, but not that big.

# 26

# This Is Your Life – On Ice

On 5 December 1995 the curtain went up on the troublesome portable ice rink that had a habit of melting in rehearsals nearly submerging the skaters, and the first-night charity audience clapped enthusiastically. I was dead tired so I watched through a stressed-out haze. All went well, the skaters were brilliant, the ice remained frozen, the reception was tremendous and as the Russians took their final bow, I was ushered with the Russian choreographer on to the stage to take a bow. Apparently this is what ballet folk do – the composer and choreographer take a bow. We walked on stage to loud applause, which was followed, oddly, by even louder applause and cheers. I looked behind me and was amazed to see Michael Aspel carrying that famous Big Red Book. He walked over to me and said, 'David Essex – This Is Your Life.'

I was dead beat and, now that the ballet was actually on, really just wanting to go home, but no, it was just like being taken prisoner. I was driven to BBC Television Centre and locked in a dressing-room. Soon a secretive make-up lady came in to stick a bit of make-up on me, then I was led to the studio. It was now about one in the morning. I couldn't believe it – all around the stage area were family and friends, including some that I hadn't seen for years.

In the past if the subject of this programme ever came up I always told Mel and Derek that I didn't want to have my life done, so the prospect of being done was something I wasn't looking forward to, but actually it was good. I had my fair share of knights of the realm putting in an appearance: Sir Tim Rice, Sir Peter Hall, Sir David Puttnam and Sir Andrew Lloyd Webber. But my favourite bit was a filmed clip of my twins, at the age of seven, running out at Upton Park with the West Ham United football team, doing tricks and scoring goals. Bill went past Rio Ferdinand like he wasn't there – it was brilliant. At the end of the recording, after many good things had been said about me, England's World Cup hero and West Ham legend Sir Geoff Hurst led the twins on.

Strangely, a few years later, Bill and Kit would actually play for West Ham's under elevens, just as I did many years ago. I was so proud when I saw them running out in their West Ham shirts to play an end of season match at Upton Park.

So, this was my life. Perhaps it should have been lives. My mentor and dear friend Derek was sadly too ill to attend the programme and declined to do a message from his hospital bed. He always had so much dignity.

Within months dear Derek died.

Derek had been in poor health for a number of years but fought it as bravely as he had fought for me. I was with him at the end, just Derek and me alone in the early hours of 1 June, and as he drifted away I softly sang the song I wrote for him, 'Friends'.

One of my regrets is that I have made many friends over the years but have almost always shied away from maintaining contact with them. I don't know if this is because I'm an only child, or if my fame has made me guarded about friendship. I do know I need a lot of space.

Throughout the Nineties there were more songs written and sung, more tours, more television. I again went to Africa, this time for Comic Relief with a motley crew of would-be footballers that included Frank Skinner, David Badiel, Nick Hancock, Angus Deayton, Ainsley Harriott, Karl Howman and John Leslie, coached and managed by football legend Terry Neill whose only team talk was 'If you see someone with the same coloured shirt pass it to them.' It was a filmed trip to spread goodwill by playing football and was called 'Balls to Africa'. Most of the team had never been to Africa before so they made me the captain. The boys coped well.

A couple of memories from that trip spring to mind. One was a night in Burkina Faso when a sand storm blew up and Terry Neill emerged in a full Lawrence of Arabia outfit. Then there was another night when we were taken to meet some village elders, and a dance ceremony was staged in our honour. The dancers were wearing fringes which went horizontal as they shimmied. Frank Skinner turned to me and said, 'Oo it's a car wash.' And this in a place where it hadn't rained for months. I tried to keep a straight face and show respect to our hosts, but it wasn't easy.

The team's greatest victory on the field was against the Ghanaian Ladies Football Team, where I was woman-marked by a player not unlike Vinnie Jones. We managed to shade it, four goals to three.

As the Nineties went on I pulled back a little from the frenzy of showbiz, and except when away for the odd adventure I was able to watch my boys grow up. I felt I had been given a second chance. With my first two children I was caught up in such a manic schedule that although I tried, I missed some of their child-hood. I was determined to do things better this time. I loved watching the boys play their sports and hanging out with them. Also, I think, after losing my father and Derek, for the first time I really began to think of my own mortality and shifted a few prior-ities, taking more time to do what I wanted, and taking more time to be with all of my children.

One event I wish Derek and Dad had been around for was my inclusion in the 1999 New Year's Honours List, when I was awarded the OBE. This stands for Officer of the Order of the British Empire or, as my kids call it, 'Old Big 'Ead'. It was a great honour to receive it and I know how proud they both would have been.

I was summoned to Buckingham Palace to receive it from Her Majesty the Queen. This in itself was a bonus, because sometimes she delegates and you get Prince Charles or someone. On these occasions you are allowed to bring three people with you to witness the ceremony, so I invited my mother, Verity and Dan.

Driving into the Palace grounds was the first thrill. I had visited the Palace twice before, once to attend a reception with Princess Anne and once to meet the Duke of Edinburgh, who was the patron of VSO; but this time, with my family beside me, it felt more special. That is until one of the attendants stopped the car and asked if I was dropping off. Mum had bought a new hat for the occasion, and Verity and Dan were suited and booted.

The award procedure is very well organized. From the souvenir point of view, an official video films you receiving the medal, official photographers record the moment when the Queen pins the medal on, and there are family portraits in the grounds after the ceremony.

When we walked into the Palace the family were led off and I was taken to the OBE enclosure. There seemed to be designated areas for the various different honours. The MBEs were in one bit – they were not quite as important as us OBEs; the Knights and CBEs had their own room. Orange juice and biscuits were laid on, and after a while we were briefed on the forthcoming investiture and points of protocol by a very high-ranking and witty Army gentleman.

I suppose we were in the enclosure for an hour or so. It was fascinating to talk to my fellow recipients, ranging from doctors who had discovered life-enhancing cures to people who had designed dams in foreign places. Their achievements were varied and very interesting; all seemed more worthy than mine.

Soon we filed one by one into a large State Room where Her Majesty was presenting the awards. Finally my turn came. I walked to the Queen, dutifully bowed, and with a few kind words Her Majesty pinned on my medal. For this patriotic man it was a great moment.

It's been and still is a wonderful and charmed life, and I am very grateful to the people who have been interested and supported what I do. I have, I think, tried to hold on to my roots, for I really feel that it's important. Recently I was asked to become Patron of the Gypsy Council, an honour which, because of my mother's background, I gladly accepted.

The aims of the Council are to promote understanding between people who travel and people who don't. It's also very active in helping with the problem of educating travelling children. The persecution of gypsies in parts of Eastern Europe is unacceptable, so I feel that having at last a representative voice for people who are isolated and at the fringes of society, is essential and worthwhile. As Mum always says, 'A land without gypsies is a land without freedom.'

Talking of freedom, I recognized quite early on that to gain creative freedom you may have to sacrifice some personal freedom. But I'm OK with that. Over the years there have been invasions into my private life that I have not liked, but generally people have been terrific to me. Having recently finished a fifty-date tour at the end of 2001, with an album called *Wonderful*, I can honestly say that the warmth and love I'm shown surprises me every time I tour. Sometimes I think I'll hang my boots up, but it seems there is always another game to play, and as long as people want me to play, I'll turn up – and, as that old football chestnut says, try to give a hundred percent. I have always tried to be honest with my work.

I am enjoying life very much now. Verity, my beautiful daughter, has just got married, in a fairy-tale wedding to her handsome 'prince'. Maybe before long I'll be a grandad – I think I'd like that. Dan I know has a big future as a record producer, Bill and Kit are becoming fine young men, and have just formed a band. I wonder if history will repeat itself? And me Mum still goes line dancing twice a week – all is good.

It's been interesting writing this book, especially as I've always tended to skip over the past in an insatiable quest to get to the future. As memories flooded back, it was strange how some felt like yesterday and some felt like part of another life. It does feel as if I have lived more than one life. I'm often told by spiritual people that I have a very old spirit that has lived many lives – well, a lot of 'em have been in this one.

In retrospect, I don't think there is much I would have changed. I am still enthusiastic with regard to writing, recording and touring, and have enjoyed doing this. Maybe a paperback writer may emerge. Who knows? In those early days when Derek and I set off in pursuit of a distant dream we had no plan, no blueprint. That's more or less the case today – I still ain't got a plan. I like it that way.

Whatever happens tomorrow, I know there will be new adventures and challenges, and more songs to write. I feel, as I have said, that I have led a charmed life, and remain grateful for the love that has surrounded me.

When I think back to those early and difficult days, to the path I walked and the hills I've climbed with the help of many creative friends, it seems amazing. I've seen the world, its injustices and its wonders. I've learned many things, but most of all I've learned to be myself. If anything I have done has touched you or made you smile, then I'm pleased. Thank you for being interested in my life. By the way, if anything I've done can serve as an inspiration to someone from 'the wrong side of the tracks', to show them you really can get from where I came from to where I got to, then I'm pleased. For now I'm off to write another album and hopefully in a few years' time, who knows, there may be another book to write…

# Index